We Not

'"Community" is one of those buzzwords that everybody from politicians to church leaders likes to use, but which lacks proper definition and content. Here is a book that provides a clear biblical content to Christian ideas of community, linking it to God's concern for justice, reconciliation and the care of creation. The author, drawing on his experience of work among the urban poor, challenges Christians to repent of their individualistic understandings of the gospel and discipleship. This is a book clearly and simply written, wise and wide- ranging in its scope. I warmly recommend it.'

Dr Vinoth Ramachandra – IFES Secretary for Dialogue and Social Engagement

'I look forward to the day when the qualification for membership of the evangelical community is not a statement of belief by an individual who has been saved but a quality of inclusive and justice-orientated communal life among a gathering of God's people. Andy Matheson challenges and inspires us to understand how this has always been God's plan, and in the process puts to the sword much of our individualistic theology and practice.'

James Featherby – Chair, Church of England Ethical Investment Advisory Group

'If the message of this book is taken seriously it will turn our lives, our churches and our society upside down. It will revolutionize our view of God, ourselves and community as well as our relationship with creation. Written out of a lifetime of experience and reflection, *We Not Me* will, on the one hand, prod and provoke you but, on the other, make you feel that you are coming home.'

Steve Chalke – founder of Oasis and Stop the Traffik

'For Andy Matheson "community" is not so much a dispassionate subject as a passionate quest, a desperate longing for connection, communication and communion carried not only by him, but by all of us, deep in our hearts as part of our DNA as human beings made in the image of God, by community, through community, for community. And the good news for us is that in his book, Andy writes about the quest for community we aspire to in a way that fires our imagination and strengthens our resolve to continue to strive for it and settle for nothing less than the one community that really matters.'

Dave Andrews – community worker, author, trainer and inspirer working with TEAR Australia

'We Not Me by Andy Matheson gives me hope – hope for the kind of change of theological perspective that the majority of Christians in the western world need if the church is to survive in their lands. For too long their theology has generally been marked by an individualistic understanding of salvation that has prevented them from seeing the wider dimensions of the gospel. As a result, they have understood the mission of the church as the way to restore the individual's relationship with God rather than as the way to lead people to fullness of life, including the transformation of their relationship with God but also of that with each other and with God's creation. Andy Matheson shows that the necessary change of

theological perspective is closely related to a renunciation of the western individualistic paradigm and the rediscovery of the centrality of community in Scripture. I wholeheartedly recommend this book.'

Dr Rene Padilla – Executive Director of Ediciones Kairos
and President Emeritus of Micah Network

'Here is a challenging and inspiring invitation to learn or perhaps learn afresh what it means to live God's kingdom here and now. If you want to explore the heart of God for our communities and with others demonstrate God's reconciling love in our world, this book will enrich your theological and practical understanding of the "how to". Micah Network is passionate about integral mission and we highly recommend this book as a key integral discipleship resource that will help readers come to grips with the radical and revolutionary lifestyle we are called to. It is intentionally written to stimulate discussion and I would recommend this book to be used in home groups and other group-discussion opportunities. However you choose to read it, you'll be challenged to be more engaged in God's mission.'

Sheryl Haw – International Director, Micah Network

We Not Me

The importance of just and inclusive relationships in an I-centric world

Andy Matheson

Authentic

First published 2014 by Authentic Media Limited
52 Presley Way, Crownhill, Milton Keynes, MK8 0ES.
www.authenticmedia.co.uk

British Library Cataloguing in Publication Data
A catalogue record for this book is available from the British Library
ISBN 978-1-78078-114-3
978-1-78078-217-1 (e-book)

Cover Design by Paul Airy (www.designleft.co.uk)
Printed and bound by CPI Group (UK) Ltd., Croydon, CR0 4YY

Acknowledgements

There are many people I would like to thank for helping me through the process of writing this book.

A number of people have kindly spent time with the manuscript at different stages and provided useful comments, questions and perspectives. These include Phil Lane, Ruth Visick-Evans, Graham Mungeam, Joel Griffith, Kevin Potter, Andrew Perry and Barrie Evans. To each of you: thank you. Special thanks go to Bob Moffett, who provided detailed input as the project neared completion, and to Mark Stibbe, who did a brilliant job in the editing phase as the book was polished and refined. A big thank you, too, to Joan, my wife, who helped with proofreading and has been hugely supportive through the whole endeavour.

I also want to thank the community of Oasis around the world. Without their support, encouragement and sense of community I would never have had the experiences that have prompted me to think deeply and reflect. The outcome of that reflection is recorded in the pages that follow.

Acknowledgements

Contents

In memory of my father,

William Matheson,

whose graciousness to all continues to be a
beacon in my life.

Introduction

When Ruthie died from an epileptic fit at the tender age of 8 her parents' pain was immeasurable.

Ruthie lived next door to us. She was a lovely child who would regularly pop in and out of our home, as would all the children in that small community. When she died her body was kept in the main room of the house, as was the local custom.

As friends and colleagues came and went over the following 48-hour period there was no expectation about how they were to behave; they didn't have to do anything or say anything. They were simply there to share the pain of the family and to express their own grief.

Every now and then Ruthie's mother or someone else might say something, or someone might pray. It was totally acceptable to question God or rant at him – nothing was off limits.

Different people would cook and meals were eaten together. Present at these meals was the growing number of relatives slowly arriving off trains and buses.

In the foothills of the Himalayas, this was how a family dealt with the excruciating loss of a loved one. The key was community: shared grief and mutual comfort, often expressed through a wordless empathy and a raw honesty.

The day that Ruthie died I learnt a lot about community. Like the vast majority of westerners I had come to view life through an individualistic lens, but this and subsequent experiences caused me to make and ultimately welcome a paradigm shift. Ruthie's death was the catalyst for seeing the world, and indeed my faith, in a new perspective and in a fresh light. It was the beginning of a radical and lasting transformation of my worldview.

As we grow older, one of the first things that changes is our eyesight. The gradual deterioration that comes with age means that we are forced to have our eyes tested and most likely learn to wear and use glasses. As the years go by, often it is necessary to have our eyes tested again and to have our lenses changed. If we are to see what's in both our immediate as well as our long-range vision, new lenses are often mandatory.

In my first book *In His Image*[1] I used this metaphor of changing lenses. I suggested that instead of using the lens of Genesis 3, viewing those outside the church as 'sinners', we need to view all people through the lens of Genesis 1 – as created in the image of God. As I wrote there, how you view a person will determine how you engage with them, and how you engage with them will have a huge bearing on the outcome of your involvement.

One of the most important consequences of embracing a Genesis 1 lens is that you understand that we are created not only for relationship with God but also for relationship with each other. In other words, we are not only made for intimate communion with the Father, Son and Holy Spirit (the vertical dimension of relationships); we are also made for authentic community with each other (the horizontal dimension). Wearing a Genesis 1 lens causes us to embrace a communal vision.

This brings me to *We Not Me*. In this book I take the idea much further and propose that community is so core to God's nature and purposes that it undergirds everything that is implied or stated on every page of the Bible. I argue that we need to embrace the perspective that God views the world through communal lenses. His vision is relational.

This truth is not easy for westerners to accept conceptually let alone apply practically. Individualism and consumerism are so pervasive that they have become the spectacles through which we view and understand our lives, including our spirituality. Sadly, we keep these glasses on as we read our Bibles, and in the process we allow our reading to reinforce our individualism.

At the church service I attended on the Sunday before writing this, we sang six songs; without exception they all used the first-person pronoun:

'O happy day, I'll never be the same.'

'In my heart and my soul, I give you control.'

'Now I've found the greatest love of all is mine.'

'Jesus, I surrender, Lead me in your ways.'

'My God is mighty to save.'

'I will extol you.'

This is not untypical of the songs that are sung in church services up and down the UK, indeed around much of the world. Since songs both reflect and shape our perspective, what we sing is very important. These songs reflect a belief that life and spirituality are individualistic. They are about 'my' relationship with God and nothing more. They express an 'I–Thou' rather than a 'We–Thou' vision. This is something we have to change.

When I was a teenager my parents gave me a copy of a compendium of Scripture readings for both morning and evening each day of the year. On the first page my father inscribed a message of love from him and my mother, quoting 2 Timothy 2:15: 'Do your best to present yourself to God as one approved, a worker who does not need to be ashamed and who correctly handles the word of truth.' Looking back I can see there was a hint of irony in this thoughtful inscription. The words, after all, urged me to be someone who would interpret the Bible responsibly. The compendium, however, was often guilty of doing the exact opposite. Many of the readings took individual Bible verses and removed them from the context in which they were written – and a text out of context can become a pretext.

Many readers and expositors of the Bible have a similar tendency to treat verses without due concern for their context. In the process, verses that were originally intended to be understood within a community setting are made to mean something different. One of the most serious consequences is that passages which refer to our community life are made to reinforce our individualism. This is not correctly handling the 'word of truth'.

When I was young, for example, I often heard evangelists quote the words of Jesus within John's vision recorded in

Revelation 3:20: 'Here I am! I stand at the door and knock. If anyone hears my voice and opens the door, I will come in and eat with that person, and they with me.' A typical evangelist would then say that the door represents our hearts and that we, as individuals, need to open them to let Jesus come in as our Saviour. No one ever questioned this interpretation and application of Scripture. It was simply accepted.

However, the truth is that the door of Revelation 3:20 is not the door of individual hearts. It is the door of a Christian community – the first-century church in Laodicea (modern Turkey). Jesus was not saying to an individual, 'Let me into your heart.' He was saying to a church, 'Let me back into your fellowship.'

Here's my point: the songs we sing and the interpretations we accept perpetuate the lie that the Christian life is all about me when in reality it's about us and them. God's purposes are focused on creating authentic community. He wants to share life with us.

This does not mean, of course, that our individual response to God or the personal decisions we make in life are unimportant. They remain of great significance. What I suggest, however, is that the weight of preaching, writing, singing and organizing within the church is so slanted towards the individual that we have lost sight of the bigger picture within which the individual response finds its place.

If we can rediscover what it means to be a community – the kind of community where all barriers are broken down and where our lives reflect the original vision of the gospel – we will play a much more effective part in ushering in God's kingdom.

That is my purpose in writing this book: to help us in our mission in the world, a mission which involves us bringing heaven to earth in places of squalor, despair and hopelessness. It's a mission to transform communities. More than that, it's a mission to transform the cosmos.

My Background

All of us come to Scripture with a unique set of lenses because of the cultural contexts in which we have been raised and the experiences of life we have had. My lenses have been shaped by the combination of a conservative evangelical upbringing and twenty years of life working in India. My conservative upbringing led me to a love and appreciation for the Bible – one that remains to this day. It also taught me to revere and cherish certain core passages in the Bible that provided assurance of God's promises and purposes for my life. My subsequent decades in India involved working among street children and those thrown out of their communities because of their HIV infection. They also led me to serve people who had been trafficked. This changed everything for me. It compelled me to look into parts of the Bible I had not really seen before. It also led me to see what I regard as the golden thread that holds the whole of the Bible together.

I had grown up understanding that that golden thread was our personal salvation. The experiences of the past thirty years, however, have caused a complete recalibration of my thinking. They have shown me that my personal response to God is a small part within a much bigger picture – a picture portraying the redemption and renewal of the whole of the cosmos. Put succinctly, I now see that the golden thread is God's plan for us all to live full and complete lives in a community in which he is pleased to dwell.

That's what this book is about. My hope and prayer is that you will read this not just on your own but in community. Discuss the questions at the end of each chapter with other people in your community. And consider changing your lenses.

1

Beginning with the End in Mind

' "Look! God's dwelling-place is now among the people, and he will dwell with them. They will be his people, and God himself will be with them and be their God. 'He will wipe every tear from their eyes. There will be no more death' or mourning or crying or pain, for the old order of things has passed away." He who was seated on the throne said, "I am making everything new!" ' – Revelation 21:3–5

As these words were read, we were standing around the graveside of a 12-year-old boy who had been abandoned as a child and had grown up on the streets of Mumbai. None of us had known little Chottu for more than six months, yet each of us had our own stories of how he had touched our lives during that time.

As we listened to these words of Scripture they filled us with hope. Hope for Chottu. Hope for ourselves and our futures. Hope that the wrongs of life would be righted one day. Hope that our deepest wounds would one day be healed.

I don't think there is a more profound promise in the entire Bible – the promise of God wiping away every tear and coming to live among us for ever. And when a community clings to these words in faith, an eternal hope can eclipse even the severest hurts.

I recently had the privilege of visiting an unusual church in Canada. I say 'unusual' but it was really what the church should always be like. Most of the church's members live on the streets or have done so in the recent past. Many of them have been in prison and have been, or continue to be, addicted to drugs. A few have had a more privileged and secure upbringing and have not experienced such poverty.

In spite of the broad spectrum of backgrounds, the truth they have discovered and which shapes how they relate to each other is the fact that we are all broken. Some of us are addicted to the life of the streets and others to work; some are addicted to drugs and others to comfort; some are addicted to alcohol and others to pornography. In this church everyone acknowledges their own brokenness and finds healing in a supportive community. I like that.

I like it because the promise of Revelation 21 is not that God will wipe away just some people's tears from their eyes; he will wipe away everyone's tears from their eyes. This means that every human soul is wounded. Every person on the earth is broken. This hope is therefore for you as well as for your neighbour. It's for street children in their throw-away rags, and it's for businessmen and -women in their tailored suits. It's for all people.

And this tear-wiping is not something that's going to happen to you in a secret, personal hideaway where just you and God meet. The setting is a public place: a redeemed community, the city of God seen by John in the visions recorded in Revelation.

God is going to dwell among us and, having dealt with the pain of our past, he is going to renew our fractured, wounded world. After that, the old earth and heavens – full of violence, disorder and injustice – are going to be recreated into something beautiful. Can you imagine that?

Think back to a time when you felt intensely close to a group of other people. Perhaps it was through a challenge that you shared with them, or a time of bereavement which brought you and them together. That experience of oneness in which there was no competition or rivalry, no mistrust or withholding, where you felt fully embraced by others: that is what the vision in Revelation 21 is about.

But it's about more than that as well. For in addition to feeling bonded to others, we are all collectively going to be bonded to God. God will be immediately present with us. He will be intimately part of us. He will dwell among us and he will dwell in us – for ever.

Strong Bonds of Community

When I first lived in India I found myself in a small community in the sprawling hillside town of Mussoorie, 2,000 metres high in the foothills of the Himalayan mountains. There were many occasions during those years when I experienced a glimpse of that oneness with others promised in Revelation. That bonding – which transcended cultural and racial boundaries – came through shared experience.

Somehow we all managed to survive everything that was thrown at us, including all the problems of running a boarding school in a remote location for 450 students of thirty different nationalities. All of us were far from home so we needed each other. Being thrown together in a cauldron of activity and challenge caused bonds to be created that have lasted to this day.

The vision of our future in the book of Revelation is one of a vibrant, healthy, loving, peaceful, fulfilled community where God is profoundly present. It's a picture of the full meaning of the word 'shalom' in the Bible (which we will explore later in this book), and everyone is invited to be a part of it. It is not the kind of divided and despairing community we see so often in the news today. Instead, it is a united and hopeful community, full of peace and promise. It is a future community which brings hope to those whose relationships are destroyed because of propaganda and prejudice. And it is a future community which brings hope to the many people who are ostracized and marginalized because of colour, gender or bigotry.

Commenting on Revelation 21 – 22 in his book *Surprised by Hope*, Tom Wright says this: 'The living God will dwell with and among his people, filling the city with his life and love, and pouring out grace and healing in the river of life that flows from the city out to the nations. There is a sign here of the future project that awaits the redeemed, in God's eventual new world.'[2] Wright goes on to make clear how this is not an abandonment of the present but a process of renewal and recreation in which we play a part. This new world will be one in which the oneness we long for in this life is guaranteed. Once there, nothing will be able to rob us of this oneness.

Most people in our world today long deep down to live in such a vibrant, loving, peaceful community where the deepest God-given desires of their hearts can find fulfilment.

The Future as a Feast

In Scripture, one of the most appealing and frequent pictures of our future life is that of a feast. Jesus pointed to this in a parable (Matt. 22:1–14) and enacted it with his disciples. 'Food will be part of the renewed creation. Food is not left behind with the resurrection. References to a future feast are not just metaphors for an ethereal future existence. Our future is a real feast.'[3] As we will see later from both the Old and New Testaments, feasting is a key part of the community life of God's people.

This comes as a shock to many today because they have embraced a quite different picture of their future – one of disembodied spirits enjoying an endless, crowded worship service. If we are honest, many of us have that picture at the back of our minds when we think of the future. If we are even more honest, we probably feel that it is quite an unattractive picture too.

The truth is, despite the fact that we don't know all the details, there is going to be continuity between our present experience and our future one, except that all injustices will have been righted and there will be nothing to prevent us from being as fully alive as God wants us to be right now. Most of us can get excited about that picture!

Oneness

Jesus pointed to this future community at the end of his high-priestly prayer – his longest-recorded prayer – in the Gospel of John: 'Father, I want those you have given me to be with me where I am, and to see my glory, the glory you have given me because you loved me before the creation of the world' (John 17:24). The central theme of this prayer is the oneness we have been talking about. Earlier in that prayer Jesus said:

> I pray also for those who will believe in me through their [the disciples'] message, that all of them may be one, Father, just as you are in me and I am in you. May they also be in us so that the world may believe that you have sent me. I have given them the glory that you gave me, that they may be one as we are one – I in them and you in me – so that they may be brought to complete unity. Then the world will know that you sent me and have loved them even as you have loved me (17:20–23).

This oneness is not simply to be a future reality; it is to be something we work at and witness today. It is to be a characteristic of our human relationships now because God's desire, as Jesus articulated it, is that the whole world should see this unity and start to experience it too.

So this oneness is not something that we will only see when the vision of Revelation 21 becomes a reality; it is something which is possible now because Jesus has given us his glory and his Spirit to help make it a reality.

Revelation 21 is accordingly an invigorating and inspiring picture of wholeness and oneness in human relationships. It is a picture of vibrant, flourishing community. It is a picture of salvation in the fullest sense of the word.

Salvation

When we see salvation purely in terms of 'my future in heaven' we are guilty of reducing this word to an individualistic and purely spiritual phenomenon. But salvation is so much more than this in the Bible. It is about the whole of life. It is about the physical as well as the spiritual. It is about the present as well as the future. God's purpose has always been for his creation to thrive, to find life in its fullness. It has never been to take individual souls to a place far away. As we will see later, it is about the restoration of shalom in the context of community. Biblically, salvation is neither merely spiritual nor merely individual. Salvation is the fulfilment of what it means to be human. It is what God always intended for his creation.

When Jesus invited himself to Zacchaeus' home, Zacchaeus' response was to promise to give half of his possessions to the poor. Zacchaeus added that if he had cheated anyone, he would pay them back four times the amount. Jesus' response to Zacchaeus was, 'Today salvation has come to this house' (Luke 19:9). If we understand salvation in a narrow individualistic sense, this seems a strange thing to say. However, if we understand salvation to be about the present, not just the future, and about well-being in all areas of life, not just in our souls, it makes total sense. Zacchaeus had just said that he was going to act justly and lovingly towards others in the community. Zacchaeus' relationships were going to be put right. As a result he would be able to enjoy loving, supportive, equitable relationships as God intended.

Perry Yoder puts it helpfully:

When we limit salvation to only a spiritual concept, when we think of salvation only as the saving of some soul which has a separate existence of its own apart from the person's total being, we no longer have a full-bodied biblical salvation, but a disembodied view of salvation. This is not how the Hebrew Scriptures talk about God's salvation, nor is it how the Synoptic Gospels talk about Jesus' saving works. Biblical salvation is liberation for the whole person, both materially and spiritually.[4]

Let me give you a picture of what this might look like. The London borough of Lambeth has some of the worst statistics of crime, violence, unemployment and alienation in the city. Within that context Oasis began work some seven years ago. It has now created a hub of activity that includes a church, school, youth club, football club, and outreach in the Accident and Emergency department of the local hospital. A couple of years ago some of those who work as part of that hub created a picture of what Waterloo might look like in the light of Revelation 21. They called it 'A New South London'. This is what they wrote:

It was 8 o'clock on Monday morning.
I was standing by Lambeth North station.
And I saw a new London coming down from the heavens.

I saw a teenager leaping out of bed with joy, laughing with the freshness of the morning.

I saw elderly ladies skipping down Kennington Road.

I saw children paddling in the River Thames.

I saw a football match in Kennington Park and the teams were mixed people from every people group: asylum seekers and taxi drivers, policemen and prisoners, pensioners and politicians. People from every race and class playing and laughing in the sun.

I saw a street party where the people were eating and dancing because there was hope again.

And I looked across the community of South London; a community of hope, a community of grace, a community of warmth.

And, in the clearness of the morning, I looked down into the Elephant & Castle and there was no more asthma, no more unwanted pregnancies, no more debt, no more violence, no more overcrowding and nobody was too busy.

The River Thames was flowing with crystal-clear water.

There were no more needles and condoms in the park.

No more sorrow or family breakdown.

No more poverty.

No more need.

No more unemployment or mind-numbing jobs.

No more hopelessness.

No more sadness and tears, only joy and laughter.

No more discrimination.

No more drunken clubbing. No threats, no fears.

The dividing walls were gone.

Families and neighbours were restored.

There was no more rubbish, no dealers, no guns, no knives, no dangerous dogs.

There were no racial tensions, just one harmonious mix in Technicolour.

And I looked and I saw kids playing football in the streets, and neighbours cheering them on.

I saw homes without locks on the doors, where a welcome was always guaranteed.

I saw a playground with climbing frames that weren't rusty, where children threw themselves in the air without fear of harm, where the teenagers helped the little ones up to the highest climbs.

I saw a London where neighbours shared favours and returned them without pressure or obligation.

I saw a London where hearts were unbroken, partnerships are lasting, peaceful and happy.

I saw a London where families eat and play together.

I saw a London where tears were wiped away.[5]

What a glorious vision!

This is the end we should keep in mind. It is the future we are moving towards. It is a picture of hope, joy and redemption. It is a picture of life without tears. It is a picture of the renewed earth.

This is the Father's endgame. It is the bookend to his book, the Bible. It is a key to understanding our purpose on the earth. For all those who, like Chottu, have unpromising beginnings, this is the ending that drip-feeds hope into even the most desperate soul. It is a source of comfort and celebration for the most oppressed and exploited person on the planet. And it is an inspiration to those who work to see justice and peace for all people who dwell on the earth today.

Questions for Community Reflection

1. Try to picture your community as part of the renewed earth. What do your street and neighbourhood look like? How does such a picture provide you with a different perspective on your lives today as a community?
2. When we understand salvation to be about now as well as the future, and about all of life not just the spiritual dimension, how does that change our message to the world?
3. How does it make you feel to realize that the future has much more continuity with the present than you may have thought (although without the presence of evil, of course)?

2

Everyone Needs Friends

'Without community people's hearts close up and die'
– Jean Vanier[6]

Shobha was one of the first women to join the community we set up near Mumbai for women and children ostracized because of their HIV status. As we travelled with Shobha on the two-hour journey out of the city to a more rural location she carried all her belongings in two plastic bags. One of these bags contained her clothes, the other a plate, a spoon and a cup. These eating utensils marked her out from the rest of her family; once her HIV status was known, she had to eat separately, using different cutlery.

As Shobha became a part of the new community which we set up she learnt that she didn't need to eat on her own with different cutlery, nor did she need to define herself according to her HIV status. She could now see herself as a unique individual created in the image and likeness of God and as part of an inclusive and empowering community. For Shobha, community was essential to her healing.

For all of us, relationships are the God-given context in which our redemption becomes real.

Having begun with the end in mind and seen the awe-inspiring vision of perfect community that awaits us, we now return to the very beginning of time, for it was 'in the beginning' that our DNA was embedded with the need for community.

Genesis 1 thrills us with this foundational truth: all people are made in the image of God. This is what makes human beings distinct from the rest of creation. All of creation is good, very good in fact, but only human beings are made in God's image. And to be made in God's image is to have that stamp of authenticity that says you are human; she is human; all of us are human.

I never realized how profound this was until we began working with street children at the railway stations in the city of Mumbai and then among others of that city who were victims of trauma. Some of the experiences people had to face beggared belief. The ways in which people overcame their difficulties were lasting demonstrations of the strength and resilience of the human spirit. All this was certainly true of Shobha. She courageously overcame the crushing alienation and exclusion that went with being an outsider even within her own home.

One of the lessons we learnt through our experiences in Mumbai was that poverty is not fundamentally about economics but about relationships. It is one thing to wear the same clothes for a month; it is another to be told you don't matter. It is one thing to beg for food; it is another to be excluded. It is one thing to have no place to rest your head; it is another to be unloved.

In this chapter we will see that community stems from the very nature of God and therefore is deeply grounded in what it means to be human. Take away relationship and you take away life.

To Be Human Is to Be in Relationship

What enabled many of those we worked among to sustain some semblance of life and dignity in the midst of horrendous circumstances were the bonds of relationship. When these did not exist people often did not survive, for without relationship life is barren. It is not worth living. It is too easy to give up, as the suicide statistics in many communities suggest. Suicide is the deepest cry from the heart of someone who feels unwanted, unknown and unloved. When the bonds of relationship are strong, people survive crisis and trauma and in some cases come out stronger.

At the core of all our hearts is a desperate need for relationship and community – to know and be known. This is because we are made in the image of God, and God's nature is relational.

If we go back to the beginning of the book of Genesis – and therefore the origin of all things – we hear God say, 'Let us make mankind in our image' (Gen. 1:26). Notice the words 'us' and 'our'. Clearly there is a conversation going on within the Godhead. If there is a conversation, there is a community. God is a community of persons, three persons in one being: the Father, the Son and the Holy Spirit. The Christian God is accordingly a relational God. As Tim Chester and Steve Timmis have written, 'The Father is the Father because he has a Son. God is persons-in-community. Human personhood, too, is defined in relational terms. You can no more have a relation-less person than you can have a childless mother or a parentless son.'[7]

When this truth is grasped it frees us to live the life that God always intended and to invest our time in what is really important. No longer do we need to worry about pensions and life insurance, cars and clothes, money and possessions; for the greatest things in life can never be possessed, only appreciated. You cannot possess community; you can only experience it. And it is for this that you and I were made. Yes, God created us to experience life in all its fullness and that life is characterized by intimate love for God and others. This is important. In fact, it is vital. Without that love we will never be able to understand the big questions of life, nor will we grasp how the Bible is held together as a canon revealing God's purposes.

As I begin to set the scene we must understand first of all, then, that to be human means to be in relationship. Secondly, human fulfilment comes through the joy of these relationships – through community. In the chapters that follow we will discuss the nature of the community that was established in the Old Testament and then in the New, and we will see the word 'community' much more clearly defined. For now, I suggest that community speaks not of geography – though we often tend to use the word in that sense – but of loving, supportive and just relationships.

Human Beings Are Image Bearers

Another implication of being made in God's image is that we've been given the mandate to image him in the world. As

part of our collective stewardship we are called to demonstrate who God is. As Doug Baker says, this mandate is
fulfilled not primarily at an individual level but in community: 'God's image is to be displayed not only in individuals,
but more fully in the interrelationships between individuals,
in the union of individuals. Only together can we display the
image of the Trinity.'[8]

Recently, my church community engaged in a re-envi-
sioning process and as part of that carried out a survey of
the people who were involved in the church. One of the
questions asked was whether people had 'a 2 a.m. friend'. In
other words, how many could call on another person for help
at any time they required it? Surprisingly, 45 per cent said
they had a friend like that; some even had several. If we do
not have anyone we can call on at any time of the day or night
for help, then, wherever we live, we do not have community.
If we do have friends like that, then, whether we live in a slum
or a mansion, an apartment block or a remote farmhouse, it
is a sign that we probably do.

The sad fact is that many individuals today feel so worthless that they live disconnected and isolated lives. Bound by a
deep-seated sense of shame, many feel that they simply aren't
worth knowing, so they start to live in the shadows, where
they can be invisible. Kathy Escobar, who co-leads an inclusive church community in Denver, reflects on this:

One of the biggest problems in every community, including
most churches, is that so many people actually feel invisible,
worthless and purposeless. They are not sure they really matter to
anyone. Stuck in shame, hiding, and feeling self-contempt, they

go through the motions of their day. Some live on the streets. Some live in apartments. Some live in nice houses. Some squeak by on social security disability income, while others collect big bonuses at their high tech company. Some use their money to buy drugs. Some use their money to buy stuff they don't need to numb their pain. Some go to church every week. Others worship other gods in different ways. Some believe in nothing, while others wonder if God has forsaken them. The problem of invisibility has nothing to do with money or religion. Invisibility has to do with our disconnectedness from the heart and soul of another human being, which then disconnects us from the reality of God.[9]

Belonging Is Key

The prevalence of gangs in western culture should not be a surprise to anyone. Gangs are inevitable where families break down, communities become divided, and where people feel that they have lost their voice and the power to change their predicament. The reason they are inevitable is because they provide an opportunity for people to belong, and belonging is core to being human. All of us need to go to bed at night knowing that, if we did not wake up, we would be missed by others. For those who are lonely and who know that they would not be missed the pain is excruciating. When young people discover that what is advertised to them as life is unattainable, they go for what is within their grasp, little knowing that the adverts are wrong and that the belonging they crave can be found without resorting to gang life.

Gregory Boyle has given his life to building a community of hope among the gangs of Los Angeles. In his book *Tattoos on the Heart*[10] he recounts hundreds of stories of young people whose lives have been for ever impacted by the gang culture. These stories are told with honesty and compassion. Some of them end well; others don't. What he has sought to do is to build an alternative community which provides a sense of kinship for the lonely. Such a community is inclusive of all – a true place of belonging for those whose scars from rejection and alienation run deep.

Jean Vanier, who set up the L'Arche communities around the world with and for people with disabilities, writes in his books about the importance of children knowing that they belong within the context of family. When that acceptance and love is not there:

> this pain can become so unbearable that the child, if it is strong enough, tries to smother it, hide it, cover it up, or forget it by directing its energies into dreams and doing things. Thus, the empty feelings of loneliness and all the pain are pushed down into the secret recesses of its being, into a sort of tomb over which a stone is rolled. All that dirt is hidden away. But with the dirt, the heart itself, the wounded heart craving for communion, is also hidden away.[11]

Intimacy Is the Reward for Openness

There is therefore a longing deep inside all people to know and be known. It is essentially a longing for intimacy. We are created for intimacy – for knowing God and knowing others in a personal and relational way.

When we know and are known by others, we are free. We are free because there is now no longer any need to impress, hide or pretend. We are accepted as we are and can therefore be at rest.

This is also to be true in our relationship with God. It is in knowing God that we begin to experience a true and lasting sense of significance and self-worth. It is in knowing God that we find acceptance and freedom. Knowing God is the only effective antidote to the shame that paralyses and isolates us. And knowing God is meant to be as intimate and real as knowing each other.

When the Bible talks of knowing God it is not talking about an intellectual reality. Knowing God is about being at rest within a relationship where nothing is hidden and where no unwanted surprises can occur.

When sin entered the world the first emotion mentioned in Genesis 3 is fear. As Adam realized he was naked, he tried to hide when he heard God walking in the garden in the cool of the day. Instead of living from a centre of love, he was now living from a centre of fear. He was ashamed, and because he was ashamed he was afraid.

Fear blocks us from intimacy with God, yet the good news is that through Christ this fear has now been overcome so that we can know and be fully known by God. We can stand before him naked yet without embarrassment or shame.

This fear can also paralyse us in our relationships with each other, preventing intimacy. Indeed, it requires extreme courage and perseverance to overcome it in order that we can reveal our true selves.

Intimacy – knowing and being known in the fullest sense – is accordingly critical for us. When we find it we discover it's a wonderful place, and it's open to all. It's part of God's purpose for our lives.

Finding Ourselves

My sister has extreme courage. When I was 12 years old she was adopted into our family as an 8-week-old baby. She was loved, accepted and treated like the rest of us. Yet life has not been easy for Rachel, and seven years ago she decided to try to trace her birth mother.

It all started when at a doctor's appointment she was asked about the health history of her family, important because of the role played by hereditary genes in many illnesses. Rachel decided to begin a search that ended with the discovery that her real mother had been forced by her parents to give Rachel up for adoption against her will when 18 years old. Rachel also discovered that she had a sister just two years younger than herself.

More important than the discovery of her medical pre-history was the discovery of that place of rest which comes from knowing who you are. It was only when she knew her history and the circumstances surrounding her adoption that she could come to terms with the rejection and reach a place of peace.

We are all made in God's image. We are all made for intimate relationships; but the greatest fear in all of us is that our desire for intimacy with others will not be reciprocated.

Among those living in isolation and aloneness close to where you live are those who don't want to be lonely; they want relationship. Some, however, have withdrawn into themselves and the last thing they want is someone to befriend them, because sometime in the past they opened their hearts up to other people and were rejected. And the pain of that is so raw, so real, that their withdrawal protects them from ever being rejected again.

Sadly, there are some like this in the church, too. They can't take down their guard or let you get too close because the scars of previous rejections run too deep. What is also sad is that those same defence mechanisms that keep others at a safe distance remain intact in their relationship with God. Yet this does not have to be the case. As people slowly open up to God and to others, healing can come and people can find that place of rest in being accepted for who they are.

My wife and I are on the same page for most things and have had the joy of working closely together in various settings around the world. However, we are very different in temperament and approach to life, and that sometimes causes conflict. As a man I often deal with that by distancing myself from my wife and going into my 'cave'. It is a natural reaction when I have been hurt, but I do it because I know it hurts her. It's my way of punishing her for something she does or says, and in her eyes it is the worst thing I can do because it destroys our intimacy. Over the years I have improved, but I still find the temptation strong when I want to send a (not very subtle) signal that I am annoyed with her. And when I cut her off in that way I am attacking her at the core of her being, because that desire for intimacy is possibly the strongest and deepest part of being human. It's that important.

Made for Community

We are made for relationship, to belong, to experience intimacy. In short, we are made for community. This is written into our DNA and is recorded on the first page of the Bible.

I love the way Jean Vanier puts it:

> When members of a community are living in communion one with another, and when the poor are at the centre of their life, the community is like a sign of the presence of God. Jesus came to reveal to humanity that God is not a solitary, eternal being, contemplating his own glory; he is not just an extraordinary Creator of a beautiful yet painful universe. God is a family of three; three persons in communion one with another, giving themselves totally one to another, each other relative to the other. And God created man and woman as a sign of the Trinity; he created them to be in communion, one with the other, in this way reflecting his Love. God yearns for community to be a sign of this communion between Father, Son and Holy Spirit.[12]

A few years ago, when William Paul Young's novel *The Shack*[13] was published, it became a source of hope for many people who had lived with a rather static and stern picture of God as Father, Son and Spirit. Young vividly portrayed the interactions between the persons of the Trinity. Within the context of a story of immense suffering Young showed the Father, the Son and the Spirit sharing together in a profound and delightful way. This resonated with millions of people because it expressed the longing in us all – to be known and to know; to give and to receive; to share in the mutuality of love.

Over recent years a number of people have rediscovered
a more radical, relational and communal reading of Scripture. This has led them to practise faith in a new way, which
is actually also an old way. New Christ-centred communities
are emerging around the world all the time and one of these
is called the New Monasticism. One of the leaders of that
movement, Jonathan Wilson-Hartgrove, says:

> The home God creates here on earth is a house of hospitality.
> Father, Son and Spirit love one another so much that they want
> to invite others into that love. They create a space where they can
> share life with people created in their image. It's a pretty incred-
> ible image of what the world was meant to be. God wanted a
> place to live together with people, so he built a home out of
> nothing and created a people. Then God told them how they
> could live the good life with him.[14]

As I read my Bible that makes much more sense than some of
the more traditional ways of understanding Scripture I have
been taught. It also makes sense of who I am.

Individual Success

Here in the UK, and indeed in much of western society, our
lives are bombarded with the idea of individual success and
achievement. Everyone is seeking to 'make it' in life, and
'making it' is determined by personal and individual achievement. We then pay homage to those who 'make it' by idoliz-
ing them, especially those who are successful in the most
public of arenas like sport and entertainment.

Prior to the 2012 London Olympics I watched a fascinating documentary on the most successful female track cyclist the world has produced – Victoria Pendleton. After winning the individual sprint gold medal in the 2008 Beijing Olympics she trained hard to repeat that success in the London Games. Her form had been up and down and the pressure to succeed was never far from her mind. What was fascinating about the documentary was the revelation that, in the midst of her rigorous training programme, she fell in love with one of the coaches but, because of team policy, had to keep it quiet. The senior coach was told but kept the news to himself until after the 2009 World Championships. When he broke the news to the other coaches they felt they had been utterly betrayed and of course, because of policy, that coach had to leave the coaching team.

I understand why a policy might exist to ensure proper professional relationships between coaches and athletes. However, as Victoria Pendleton talked to camera about the ups and downs of her life, it was clear that what gave her life real meaning and joy was not the pursuit of another gold medal but the affirmation and fulfilment that came from her relationship. Individual success is what society honours and idolizes, but relationship and community are what we are created for.

When Jesus told the rich young ruler to sell his possessions, give to the poor and come and follow him (Luke 18:18–30), his invitation was not to an individual and isolated spirituality. His invitation was to join a community; to become a fellow disciple with all the others; to learn within the context of life relationships. If we read this passage through the lens of our individualistic culture we can misguidedly think that God's invitation is simply personal and that true spirituality is about me and my faith. The truth is that authentic discipleship and spirituality are discovered and developed most potently through community.

In John 17 Jesus' prayer for his disciples was for their 'oneness'. This joining of people together was to replicate the joining of the Father and the Son. That's the goal. That's the place God wants to get us to. That's the prayer of Jesus. And through such 'oneness' everyone will be drawn to see, to believe and to join the ever-widening circle of God's community on earth.

Questions for Community Reflection

1. What strikes you most about the meaning of being made in the image of God? Share your response with others in your group.
2. Does your church community or group invest in building loving, supportive relationships, or do people get sucked into investing their time in other things that reflect the priorities in the world to own and to consume?
3. Do you have deep, meaningful and intimate relationships with other people? What prevents you if you do not?

3

God's Big Idea

'The people who find God are usually people who are very serious about their quest and their questions, more so than being absolutely certain about their answers' – Richard Rohr[15]

The last vacation my wife and I took prior to having children was a trip to the Kashmir Valley in northern India. At the time we were living at around 2,000 metres high in the foothills of the Himalayan mountains. It was a stunning location. During the summer break we, along with some friends, decided to ride our Enfield 350cc motorbikes from Mussoorie westwards through the Himalayan range. It took us seven days to reach Jammu and from there we had a two-day ride along a 350 kilometre-long road into the Kashmir Valley.

All went well until we reached a tunnel not far from our destination that was 2.7 kilometres long. As we entered it, it didn't take us long to realize that we were in for a challenge. First of all, there were no lights in the tunnel. Secondly, the lights on our bikes were limited in their effectiveness because of the smog caused by the buses and lorries that had gone ahead of us. Thirdly, the road had groove marks in it from constant use by four-wheel vehicles. Fourthly, the potholes were all covered over by water from leaking pipes.

As I could not see even a metre in front of me I slowed down to a snail's pace, only to have a lorry come breathing down my neck from behind. It was not a place for anyone with claustrophobia!

The reason we eventually made it through alright was that on the left-hand side there was a railing, so I managed to navigate by looking to my left and keeping a constant distance from it. As we emerged from that tunnel, the ordeal was immediately put into perspective by the most stunning view we had ever seen in our lives. Before us lay the panoramic beauty of the Kashmir Valley, breathtaking in its greenery.

In many ways, emerging into a new understanding of the Bible and God's purposes revealed there has been for me like emerging from that tunnel. The claustrophobic sense of a narrow story relevant for a few select people has been replaced by a panoramic vision of the vastness of God's purposes for all creation. A story that seemed to be only about the spiritual dimension I now see to be about the whole of life because, as stated by the title of Rob Bell's recent tour, 'Everything is spiritual'. A story that seemed to provide good news only for the future I have now come to see as good news for the present as well. Though the revelation has come to me over a period of time, the impact has been like balm to my soul as my eyes have been lifted up to the wonder of all that God is and all that he is doing.

My Early Years

I grew up in the wonderful simplicity of a church environment where faith was real, things were clear and where every question had an answer. It was not difficult to want to imbibe the kind of faith espoused by some of the adults I had the privilege of rubbing shoulders with. Many of them were gracious and generous people, and when at the age of 22 I went off to India I was pretty sure that I had been groomed well to share those same answers with those who came looking. There had been a brief period of 'rebellion' but thankfully all had been forgiven and the experience gained meant I had just a little bit more of an induction into the ways of the world.

I look back on those years with great affection, even though they were not straightforward. In some ways I long to return to their simplicity and to the black-and-white world that existed in my head, but I know I cannot do that. Something has apprehended me and I do not want it to let go, nor can I let it go.

That something began to stir over twenty years ago as I came face-to-face with the reality of life for so many of the world's poor. This confrontation meant that I would either have to abandon my faith or return to the Bible with different eyes.

I chose to take off my old lenses – the lenses belonging to a middle-class white male with an individualistic understanding of life. I decided to re-imagine my faith.

There are those who think that people who re-imagine their faith are somehow taking Scripture less seriously. I believe, however, that the opposite is true. It is precisely because so many people today are trying to take the Bible more seriously that we are asking questions that demand a greater level of transparency and honesty. It is because we have such a high view of Scripture that we are letting it make a fresh demand upon us – one that will shake us out of a narrow view into a more open space where true community can be found.

This kind of language does, however, upset people who still operate with old, individualistic lenses. They tend to react by saying, 'You were conservative but you're now a liberal.' 'You used to believe the Bible, but now you're just one of those woolly, social-justice people.'

But this is not about changing from a conservative to a liberal view of the Bible: it's about rigorously seeking to find its truth and to live obediently in the light of that truth, whatever the cost.

An Individualized View of the Bible

As I grew up I unconsciously imbibed a framework for understanding how the whole of the Bible was held together. Those who taught me would look at different passages but fundamentally everything came back to the same theme – me and my relationship with God. The framework that I developed in my mind was primarily about what my response to God was going to be. You could summarize the Bible in a paragraph like this:

'God created a perfect world. It all went very wrong very quickly with the entry of sin. God then modelled through his relationship with Israel how they needed to deal with sin – it was about sacrifice. However, the blood of bulls and goats didn't change people's hearts; it simply pointed to the coming of someone who would deal with sin properly. A whole range of people prophesied the build-up to the coming of Christ and although when he did come people didn't recognize him as the one to deal with sin, he did deal with sin. His death sorted the problem out. As I put my trust in him my personal sin is forgiven. What is more, the Holy Spirit then enters my life to empower me to live a holy life and to tell other people of what Jesus has done so that they can join me in heaven one day and not go to hell.'

This may seem like a caricature, but it is close enough to the message that was constantly communicated.

I lived with that framework for many years and tried my hardest, like many others, to be as perfect as I could, since the Bible encouraged me to personal moral perfection. It also motivated me to get others to say a prayer of repentance so that they could join me in striving for perfection in this life while having the insurance policy of ending up in heaven.

As I look back I realize how much I had taken on board the British evangelical approach to faith that was individualistic, regarded sin as the central human problem, focused only on the spiritual dimension, and was concerned much more with my future destination than my current circumstances. Within that framework of faith there was nothing about the poor, justice or community, nor a myriad of other causes and concerns that are central within the Bible.

The Challenge to Find a New Framework

I then went to live and work in the foothills of the Himalayas and then in Mumbai, and because of those experiences I

started to read the Bible differently. In fact, I started to realize
that the framework I had grown up with, though it contained
a lot of truth, seemed to ignore vast areas of the Bible. It was
as if all I had really needed before were a few small sections
from it, not the whole book.

Once I had worked among the poor, however, I was forced
to try to discover what the Bible had to say that was 'good
news' for a street child, or for a girl who had been trafficked
into prostitution, or for a lady who had been thrown out of
her community because of her HIV status.

Many others have been, or are on, that journey too. Scott
McKnight puts it well:

> Let's all admit something: the enormity of the task makes a
> much smaller gospel, one tailored for individuals, so much more
> attractive. It would be easier to promise forgiveness from sins
> and heaven when we die. But that is the one thing Jesus tells us
> in his kingdom vision that we cannot let happen. As followers of
> Jesus we are stuck with a big gospel with a big claim.[16]

One of the problems for those of us who are seeking to
remain faithful to Scripture while trying to understand its
relevance to those who are oppressed and poor is that we need
a new framework to replace the old. The old framework was
a framework of personal faith that ignored large sections of
the Bible. This old framework also took individual verses and
made them prescriptive truths detached from the context in
which they were written.

Let me give you an example. Romans 3:23 would often be
quoted to determine the fact that everyone is a sinner: 'for all

have sinned and fall short of the glory of God'. While that statement can be understood as one about personal sin, this isn't what Paul was talking about. If you look at the context, Paul's point was that there is no advantage being a Jew or being a Gentile. Both are in the same boat. Paul was simply using the fact of common sin to illustrate this point. In fact, far from being a statement about personal sin, this is a statement about universal sinfulness.

This becomes even more evident and significant when we remember what the whole of the letter of Romans is about. Those who employ the old framework claim that its core message is that through faith in Christ and his atoning work I can find personal salvation. However, if you make that the central message you have to leave out large sections about ethnic groups, specifically Jews and Gentiles – sections which paint on a canvas that's bigger than just my personal need of Christ. If, however, we understand this letter to be about Jews and Gentiles living together as God's new community (that is to say, the church), it makes much more sense. Verses like 'all have sinned' are no longer personal statements; they are social and cultural statements. 'Everyone has sinned,' Paul exclaims. 'Jews can't claim to be exempt and Gentiles can't continue to be in denial. Everyone's on the same level playing field. Every social group, every community, every tribe, every race, needs salvation.'

Does embracing the new framework mean that my personal response to Jesus is unimportant? Of course not! As I said in the Introduction, the individual response that people make to the claims of Christ and the invitation to follow him is vitally important. What I am suggesting, however, means that I understand my salvation in a much wider perspective and as part of a much grander purpose.

When I become a Christian, it's not so that some spiritual part of me will live for ever when I go to heaven after I die. When I become a Christian, I become a part of a community that's dedicated to bringing heaven to those who are experiencing hell on earth. This is why we need to critique the old lenses and the old framework.

When we understand the Bible from the narrow perspective of our individual relationship with God we end up focusing on a few key verses rather than the big story of God's engagement with the world over time. When we grasp that God's purposes are truly cosmic the biblical text comes alive as we grapple with what that means for his mission in our world today and our part in it.

A Different Paradigm

The Bible is not easy to understand. That should not surprise anyone, considering it was written in many different contexts by many different authors. It also contains a range of different types of writing, from straight historical recollection to poetry and even a genre called 'apocalyptic writings'. It contains people's views as well as some direct revelations from God and holds contradictions that have provoked theologians over many years to disagree with each other.

If we are going to interpret the Bible responsibly, our reading of it has to be informed by what the original authors intended and by how the original readers would have understood what they were reading. As many theologians say, context is therefore vitally important. The original authors of the Bible were members of a community writing for a community (or communities) and very often about community. Our readings and interpretations should therefore not ignore the social context of Scripture.

Simply taking the words of Scripture and interpreting them through the individualistic lens of western culture will lead us to a place far from the one God intended. Yet I am afraid that this is exactly what has happened. We have taken much of what Jesus and Paul said and applied it to ourselves individually. That has led us to emphasize 'personal faith', making a 'personal decision' and having a 'personal walk' with God.

If you ask a person today in a western context how things are going, their response will be based on their own emotional state and what measure of success or failure they have experienced in recent days as individuals. If that same question was put to a Jew in Jesus' day they would respond with a description of how their family and community were doing. In his book *Old Testament Ethics for the People of God* Chris Wright explains that westerners tend to start with the individual and work towards community, whereas a Hebrew would begin with community and would then work out the individual application. He says, 'It is my contention . . . that the individual aspects of Old Testament theology and ethics cannot be appreciated apart from an understanding of the community God called into being.'[17]

At this point I realize that there is a risk of my being misunderstood and being accused of dismissing individual decision-making or choice as irrelevant. I do not want to do that. Throughout the Bible there is ample evidence that personal choice is important and that people make many decisions that are crucial in the acceptance and development of faith. What I am suggesting here is not that individual choice is unimportant but rather that it is not the be-all and end-all of God's wider purposes. When we grasp this, the priority then becomes seeing God's big picture and purposes and choosing to make right decisions in the light of that. That, of course, is a major challenge and one we will explore later.

The Bible's Central Message

As a result of both my journey and my study I believe the central framework of the Bible is this: *God wants all people to experience fullness of life. That fullness comes when people live in loving, supportive, equitable and just relationships with each other while God is present among them by his Spirit. In other words, God's purposes are all about 'community'.*

We saw in Chapter 1 that this is our final destination: a place where God dwells among us in completeness while all that causes pain and heartache is gone and we can relate to each other as God's people who truly love each other as we love God. In Chapter 2 we then went back to the beginning in Genesis 1, where we found that we are created for relationship and that belonging and intimacy are written into our DNA. In the beginning God dwelt with Adam and Eve, walking in the garden as they enjoyed each other in the beautiful surroundings that God had made. Genesis 1 and Revelation 21 are the bookends of the Bible and both speak about community.

As we begin in the coming chapters to look at what is contained in the Bible between these two sections we will explore how 'community' provides a framework for us to understand the whole of the Bible. As Scott McKnight puts it:

> The gospel, you will recall, is the work of the triune, inter-personal God – a God in whom community is essence. And humans are made in God's *eikon* [image] with a relationally pointed compass. If the direction of this gospel compass is union with God and communion with others, then we can be 're-unioned' with God and 're-communioned' with others. Which means this – and I know this may sound edgy to some: the gospel is designed to create community out of individualists.[18]

The Amazing Breadth of Salvation

I am not the only one to have attempted to articulate the flow of the Bible story from Genesis to Revelation, especially with regard to God's engagement with the whole of creation. In *The Drama of Scripture* Craig Bartholomew and Michael Goheen focus on the theme of king and kingdom using a plan involving six acts – creation, sin, Israel, Jesus, mission and new creation. Towards the end of their book the authors reflect on the breadth of God's involvement with creation:

> Salvation is not an escape from creational life into 'spiritual' existence; it is the restoration of God's rule over all creation and all of human life. Neither is salvation merely the restoration of a personal relationship with God, important as that is. Salvation

goes further: it is the restoration of the whole life of humankind and ultimately of the non-human creation as well. This is the scope of biblical salvation.[19]

I say 'Amen' to that.

It is interesting that in the Old Testament the main image for understanding God's salvation is the experience of the people of Israel as they escaped slavery and suffering in Egypt, in particular at the hands of Pharaoh. They were saved from real physical and emotional abuse at the hands of other people. It is interesting to note that, in recent years, being rescued from violent abuse is not even considered an aspect of salvation, let alone a central aspect.

Some people have reflected on how we managed to reduce the all-encompassing purposes of God and shrink them down into something future-orientated and simply personal. Perry Yoder believes it was because sin became the central issue. He writes:

The forgiveness of sin and the restoring of relationship with God so that one would go to heaven became the focus of the church and was referred to as being saved. Thus salvation became an individual, interior, spiritual, and future matter. What had earlier been treated as salvation – liberation from physical ills and social oppression – thus fell outside the church's notion of salvation. As a result, it was not seen as central to the church nor something to which the church should devote major energy and attention.[20]

I believe that the core purpose of God that holds not only the whole of Scripture but also our lives together is about 'community'. 'Our relationships of humble, purposeful, open, vulnerable love are intended to mirror the loving relationships within the Trinity. Indeed, throughout the Bible we see that, though God does call individuals to love and obey him, his desire is to make a people, to create a community.'[21]

The Genesis of Individualistic Faith

How did we arrive at such an individualistic paradigm of faith? James Thwaites suggests that our problems are rooted in the fourth century BC with Greek philosopher Plato's view that the real world is a spiritual one which cannot be seen, in contrast to the physical world where life is lived.[22] James Torrance blames Roman philosopher Boethius in the late fifth and early sixth centuries, and identifies 'a static concept of the individual as a substance possessing three faculties (reason, will, emotion), with primacy given to reason'.[23] This concept had a big influence on the development of western theology and led to the belief that 'God's primary purpose for humanity is legal, rational, individualistic'.[24]

We should not forget the impact of the Age of Reason (the Enlightenment), either. This caused the church to develop rational defences for Christian truth. This in turn led to the church articulating its faith through the use of apologetics – a method designed to help an individual grasp truth.

Tom Wright suggests that those who endorsed the Enlightenment as the turning point in history had to then show that the coming of Christ could not also be the turning point. That created a separation between religion and politics, which meant that the development of faith became a personal and private matter while the realm of politics became the domain of the state. As he says, 'The gospel message is substantially neutralized as a force in the world beyond the realm of private spirituality and an escapist heaven.'[25] Walter Brueggemann says, 'It is obvious that the churches which historically have thought of sin, guilt and forgiveness in a narrow sense have settled for a very individualistic articulation of the gospel.'[26] When the Christian life becomes focused on what we believe, it is natural for our attention to turn from community to the individual.

The Peak of Individualism

It is hard not to believe that we have now reached the apex of individualism with the creation of stars and celebrities. This is so prevalent in the UK today that when children are asked what they want to be when they grow up, they often say, 'A celeb'. 'Celebs' appear in all walks of life, from football to cooking, and are what young people aspire to be.

Such individualism has greatly impacted the church. For example, we have created Christian celebrity worship leaders and celebrity pastors of mega-churches. The issue is not with those considered such but with our culture that wants to create them.

Looking at faith from a more communal standpoint is vital if we are to be God's people in the western individualized culture of our day. When we simply reflect our culture and do not shape it, we lose our prophetic role in the world. I fear that, as the church, we have bought into our individualized, materialistic and consumer-orientated culture to the extent that we are somewhat numb to considering alternatives.

As I mentioned in the Introduction, individualistic spirituality is sadly reflected even in our corporate worship. This is something we have to change. The sad thing for us all is that when individualism gets a grip on our lives we miss so many of the good things of life as it was intended. For example, we think that God will speak to us directly and often in a context we consider 'spiritual'. Doing that means that we can miss God in the ordinary events of community life. 'The Word of God calls us to discover the person and presence of God in each other. To feel and know the friendship of God in the fellowship of a brother or sister. To enjoy the romance and love of God in the embrace of a wife or husband. To sense the tenderness of God in holding a child close.'[27]

It is vitally important we remember that, although culture and context change, the nature of being human does not. Just as in the days of the Old Testament and in the days of Jesus, so today relationship and community remain central to our very DNA. 'The human person is someone who finds his or her true being in relation, in love, in communion.'[28]

The big challenge, then, is this: how do we take a communal view of Scripture and the truth that would have been contextually understood by the disciples of Jesus and the early church and appropriate it for our very own in our day? That is something we will come to a little later.

First, though, there is one more important point to mention. The interpretive lens of community now helps us to hold the whole of Scripture together, without having to view some parts as disconnected or secondary. When we look at the

Bible through the old paradigm of personal salvation there are vast sections of Scripture that seem irrelevant. However, when we grasp that God's purpose is for all people to live lives of wholeness and fullness in the context of community while he is present among them, there isn't a part of Scripture that is irrelevant. Personal salvation fits within a much wider framework that encompasses God's redemption and renewal of the whole cosmos.

Questions for Community Reflection

1. What questions and concerns do you have whenever the individualized perspective of faith and salvation is challenged? How might these be addressed?
2. What excites you about the possibility that community might be a central theme which helps us to understand the whole of the Bible?
3. Share some of the paradigm shifts you have had over the years with respect to how you understand God's work in the world.

4

From Brick-Making to Feasting

'Character ethicists say integrity of character is shaped when we see ourselves, our lives and our loyalties as part of a larger drama that shapes our community' – Glen Stassen and David Gushee[29]

Ever since Swapna had been abandoned by her parents she had served the greed of a man who now controlled her. She was not the only one, for when Swapna was rescued she led our team and the accompanying police to seven other victims who were all likewise under this man's control. They were living in a structure made out of bamboo poles and plastic sheeting, yet they spent little time there. Instead, their mornings started early as they were sent out to beg at key points in the city, where daily commuters were faced with the choice to give or not. Some ignored the children while others gave without realizing that their small change would not benefit the children but their slave master. Like so many others, Swapna was slowly being robbed of her childhood.

An operation coordinated by the Bangalore police and the Child Welfare Committee – in partnership with several

NGOs, including Oasis – rescued over a hundred such children. Swapna was one of them. One day she was a slave, the next, she was free. She represents the millions of slaves who lie hidden within homes and businesses and on the streets of our towns and cities throughout the world.

Slavery is alive and well. It has always existed and, sadly, wherever there is greed it will continue to do so.

Escape from Slavery

Slavery formed part of the history of God's people Israel. Having gone up to Egypt to escape a famine, the descendants of Jacob ended up settling there and over time were enslaved by the Egyptians. The land that originally saved them became the location of their greatest suffering. Yet it was not to be the end, for their rescue became the defining event in their history. God was getting ready to intervene and to act. He was preparing a plan of salvation that would result not just in the people escaping their misery, but in them having an opportunity to organize their lives as a community on the principles of justice, peace and equity.

As Scripture reveals, the road that lay ahead of them to the Promised Land was a tortuous one, made more difficult by their hardness of heart and their failure to grasp God's good purposes towards them.

Within this period of waiting and wandering they were given the basis of how to live in the Ten Commandments. These were prefaced with a reminder that it was God who had brought them out of slavery, a fact it seems God wanted to engrave on their consciences. In fact, throughout the Old

Testament God frequently reminded Israel of their liberation. Part of the reason for these reminders had to do with the call to Israel to appreciate their freedom, but an even more important part had to do with Israel not becoming oppressors themselves. God's primary purpose in reminding Israel of their deliverance and salvation was so that they would not turn from oppressed to oppressor – a journey that can be made all too easily. Instead, they would become a people who would model all the ideals and principles of what it means to live a full and complete life in relationship with each other and with God. In modelling what community is, with God's all-important presence among them, other nations would look and see and ultimately realize God's good purposes for all people. As Jonathan Wilson-Hartgrove puts it, 'God wants Israel to show the whole world what it looks like to really live.'[30]

The Ten Commandments: Guidelines for Community Living

The Ten Commandments must be seen within this context. They are not the prohibitions of a holy God, as they have sometimes been perceived. Rather, they are a framework for building a healthy community. Four of the commandments are primarily focused on the relationship that the people have with God and six are primarily focused on the relationship that people have with each other. In fact, such a division into four and six may not be that helpful. It is probably more accurate to say that all ten are focused on the relationship people have both with each other as well as with God.

For example, in Exodus 20:8–11 the indication is that the Sabbath is something to be kept for God but, as we enter the New Testament and Jesus' disciples are caught breaking this commandment, Jesus' response is that the commandment was made for the benefit of people (Mark 2:27).

Likewise, our first response to the commandment regarding idols (Exod. 20:4–6) is that it is focused on how people relate to God. In reality, however, because we become like that which we worship, when people create idols it has huge implications on their relationships with others. Richard Rohr says, 'The genius of the first commandment was that by putting "one God before you", you were placed inside one coherent world, with one center, one pattern, one realm of meaning.'[31] The grand purpose was for Israel to live life to the full, something epitomized by the concept of shalom – a concept we will study in more depth in the coming chapters.

I suggest that all ten of the commandments and all the detail that follows in the books of Leviticus and Numbers have this same agenda: they are there for the benefit of people. This appears to be Jesus' take on it when he says, 'So in everything, do to others what you would have them do to you, for this sums up the Law and the Prophets' (Matt. 7:12). Reflect on those words: the whole Law and all that the prophets said to the wayward people of Israel can be summed up in doing to others what they would want done to them.

So the Ten Commandments are relational. They are about how all human beings can live lives of wholeness, fullness and completeness in the context of community. As Chris Wright says, 'God's purpose . . . was not to invent a production line for righteous individuals, but to create a new community of

people who in their social life would embody those quali-
ties of righteousness, peace, justice and love that reflect God's
own character and were God's original purpose for humanity.'[32]

The Narrow Way

I have a hunch that this is what Jesus was alluding to when
he talked about the narrow path. That section flows straight
on from Jesus' summing up of the Law and the Prophets in
Matthew 7 (vv. 13,14). Perhaps the narrow path has nothing
to do with eternal destiny but everything to do with fullness
of life today – the narrow path being the one where we treat
others as we would like to be treated: with justice, peace,
dignity and equity. That path leads to fulfilment for all. It's a
hard path to get onto because it is about escaping individualism.

It's about not using your position for personal gain. It's
about not seeking to trample over others in the game of life.
Those are easier, more natural paths to take, but they end in
destruction. True life, however, comes from putting others
ahead of you; from taking the lowest place; from seeking the
welfare of your community, not your own.

Gregory Boyle makes an interesting point about Jesus'
reference to the narrow path as it relates to the way people
view themselves and particularly those whose lives have been
shaped by the ghetto in his book *Tattoos on the Heart*. He
suggests that the narrow way is not about restriction but focus
and that as we focus we will find the way opening up before us
as we discover God's broad and expansive purposes.[33] Surely

this is true. Those who do focus on personal gain, position and obtaining power never find themselves in that expansive place but instead are so often consumed by the fear of loss. Those who live their lives for the benefit of others have nothing to lose and so are free. This leads to life because life is found in what we contribute, not in what we consume. When Jesus said, 'It is more blessed to give than to receive' (Acts 20:35) it wasn't another command or demand; it was simply a reflection on the nature of what it means to be human. Ultimately, receiving, obtaining or having do not fulfil the deep desires of the heart; only giving and seeking the welfare of others can do that. This is what the narrow way is about.

God's Desire to Share in the Life of His People

As the people of Israel were being formed into a loving, supportive community that would bless the nations of the world, God made it clear that his desire was to share his life with them. He wasn't interested in looking on from a distance while they tried to obey him; he wanted to be among them.

That's what the tabernacle was all about. Its purpose wasn't so that God could keep an eye on them; it was so that he could enjoy being among them. As the people of Israel made their way from Egypt to the Promised Land the tabernacle would accompany them, and this tabernacle would be the place of God's dwelling. As God said to Moses, 'let them make a sanctuary for me, and I will dwell among them. Make this tabernacle and all its furnishings exactly like the pattern I will show you' (Exod. 25:8,9). What follows is some elaborate detail about every aspect of what the tabernacle would be like and contain, including the ark, the table, the altar and the ephod. 'There I will meet you and speak to you; there also I will meet with the Israelites,' God said (Exod. 29:42,43). He then went on to reiterate that the very reason he brought the people out of slavery in Egypt was so that he could dwell among them and be their God (29:45).

A little further on in the book of Exodus, following the incident with the golden calf, Moses asked God whom he would send with him to lead the people into the Promised Land. God's response was, 'My Presence will go with you, and I will give you rest' (Exod. 33:14). Such assurance led Moses to ask to see God's glory, a request God granted as he passed by a cleft in a rock. Again it is clear that God desires closeness with his people and to share their lives. He desires to be present among them rather than act as a distant God demanding obedience for obedience's sake.

God's desire to live among his people is made clear in so many ways in his interactions with Israel: not just through the creation of the tabernacle and then the temple, but also in the covenant he made with them and through the words spoken by the prophets. As Tom Wright says, 'This pattern – God intending to live among his people, being unable to do so because of their rebellion, but coming back in grace to do so at last – is, in a measure, the story of the whole Old Testament.'[34]

Fundamentally, all those parts in Exodus, Leviticus, Numbers and Deuteronomy that we tend to skip over pretty quickly point us to God's twofold purpose for Israel and, through them, for the world. The first part was that Israel should live as a wholesome, fulfilled, loving and just community. The second was that God would dwell among them.

This is what the commandments were about; it's what all the detail of the Law was about; it's what the covenant was about; it's what the prophets continually pointed to when things went wrong and didn't work as God had intended.

What This Means for Us

This is important because so many Christ-followers I know have lived their lives on the basis that the commandments are individual moral prohibitions that God has literally set in stone. They are there, so these people think, to stop certain forms of behaviour; when broken, they fuel God's frustration and anger with us. It is no wonder that despite what we read in the gospels, if this is the framework for understanding the commandments, we will all live lives of worry and fear. Instead, I suggest, the commandments must be seen as guidelines for a community so that all people can enjoy the quality of life that God intended: where people don't get left out and where fairness and justice mark all relationships. Ultimately, the commandments were not given to keep us in check but to help us live fulfilled lives.

When parents allow their children into the garden to play but tell them to avoid the thorn bush near the fence and the pond at the end of the garden, they are doing so because they want their children to have a great time. That is what the commandments are about. They are relational. They are for our benefit.

When this truth sinks deep into our hearts and we begin to enter through the narrow gate we find it is indeed the gate into an expansive world. The easy path is to look out for ourselves and do our own thing. The hard path is to think about others and do for them what we would want done to us. The hard path is the community path. It's the path that means everyone prospers. It's the path that ushers in God's presence. For his desire is to dwell among us and share our lives.

Questions for Community Reflection

1. How do you view the commands in the Bible? How do things change when you view them as given so that your community can prosper?
2. How does seeing the narrow way as the entry into the expansive realm help change your view of God's purposes for you and your community?

5

A Second Chance

'I desire mercy, not sacrifice' – The Bible[35]

My favourite show at the theatre is *Les Misérables*. When I see it in London's West End I find the quality of the set, music and songs breathtaking. Yet it's the story that grabs your heart, a story of someone given a second chance.

Jean Valjean steals from a priest and is arrested, but the priest gets him released and through that one act of kindness Jean Valjean realizes both his brokenness and his capacity for good. So he makes good and takes care of others, specifically the daughter of a woman whose only means of providing for her is by working as a prostitute.

There is much more to the story than that, but the point here is that Jean Valjean receives kindness and as a result then demonstrates kindness to others. Having been liberated from his oppressors, he seeks to liberate others from their oppression.

Israel's Failure

With the people of Israel having been rescued from slavery you would think they would have realized that justice, peace and equity were foundational to establishing their new community in the Promised Land. Yet they just could not 'do to others what [they] would have [the others] do to [them]' (Matt. 7:12), to use the words of Jesus when summarizing the Law. The powerful couldn't avoid exploiting those who were weak. Those who were rich didn't share their wealth with the poor. People got left out – the orphans, widows, foreigners and strangers. Once you were at the bottom of the ladder there was little chance of getting back the source of wealth creation, not least because the laws of land redistribution were not being obeyed. This was not as God had intended. Some of the oppressed who had been saved by God out of Egypt now became oppressors themselves, and of their own people too.

But that wasn't all. At the same time as God's people failed to do those things that would ensure that fullness of life was experienced by all, they carried on with all the outward symbols, rituals and festivals that actually reminded them of God's call to share their lives and be present among them. They carried on fasting, feasting, tithing and gathering, while at the same time many among them were being exploited. And God was upset – very upset. You can understand why, because his purpose was that as they lived in loving, support- ive relationships with each other, all the other nations would realize that YAHWEH was God and would see modelled before them the way to live.

God gave Israel not just a second chance, but also a third, fourth and many more to put this right. In fact, God never stopped encouraging them to live as he intended, nor provid- ing them with opportunities to do so. He sent prophets to remind them of his desires. He also gave way to some of their demands, hoping that in doing so they would finally learn and change. Yet change never came and so God allowed his people to be sent into exile in the hope that finally, when they reached rock bottom, they would realize their mistake and would turn to him for help. In the process they could restart God's project of modelling what it meant to live as a loving, just and supportive community with God present in their midst, sharing their lives.

God Sends Messengers to His People

One of the prophets whom God sent to his people during their exile was Zechariah. In the midst of his short prophetic book we discover a wonderful picture of community – a place of safety, joy and relationship where everyone, from the youngest to the oldest, finds their place. The children are able to play and the elderly are able to sit outside and watch all that goes on, knowing that the generation to come will savour the bonds of community as much as they have done (Zech. 8:4,5). This beautiful picture is illustrative of God's purpose for his people Israel, and through them, for all the peoples of the earth.

The context of Zechariah's prophecy is that the people are in exile in Babylon and Darius is king. They have been there for seventy years (Zech. 1:12) and are at last coming to realize that what has happened is what they as a people have deserved. This realization, however, doesn't seem to change how they behave because two years later, when they enquire through the priests whether they should continue their usual habit of fasting (7:3), God responds by pointing out that their motivation for fasting is selfish, just like their motivation for feasting. Then comes what can only be described as a broken record as far as God is concerned. He has said this to the people so many times before, you would have thought that what he desires of them would be blindingly obvious. But no, it isn't! 'Administer true justice; show mercy and compassion to one another. Do not oppress the widow or the fatherless, the foreigner or the poor. Do not plot evil against each other' (7:9,10). A little later God repeats some of this: '"These are the things you are to do: Speak the truth to each other, and render true and sound judgment in your courts; do not plot evil against each other, and do not love to swear falsely. I hate all this," declares the Lord . . . "Therefore love truth and peace"' (8:16–19).

These words are repeated over and over throughout the Old Testament as time and again God urged the people to live lives of justice, inclusion, truth, grace and wholeness. Zechariah is therefore not an obscure little book that can be sidelined as a one-off. Its message is repeated throughout the Old Testament and is core to everything God wanted for his people. The idea of fairness, equity and justice was not an add-on to God's purposes. It wasn't something to consider as an extra to other, more 'spiritual' activities. It was God's master plan. It was what it meant to follow him. It was absolutely central.

All the things that are mentioned in those verses – speaking truthfully, being compassionate, delivering sound judgements and not thinking evil of others – are crucial components in the life of a community. When these things are present people get on well, those on the edges are included, everyone returns home from a day of productive work and eats a decent meal, and those who suffer from poor health are cared for by those who are strong and able. This is what God wants: people to live lives of productivity, joy, fulfilment and wholeness.

Living by Form but Losing the Spirit

What had happened to the people of Israel is what often happens when people live by the form but lose the spirit. The question they asked of the priests gives it away. Should we mourn and fast as we have done for so many years? Such questions betray the distance the people had travelled from God's original good purposes for them. These were not onerous tasks given by a God who wanted to be remembered; neither were they tasks to fuel obedience to a God who wanted to be obeyed. They weren't road blocks; they were aids to a full life. But when the spirit is lost and only the form is left, people will naturally ask about the relevance of any practice. And that's exactly what they did here.

God said to the people that they should forget the mourning and fasting and do the things that the mourning and fasting were there to produce – demonstrating justice, mercy, compassion and proactive love towards those who couldn't take care of themselves. Fasting and feasting were activities that existed to constantly remind people of God's goodness and provision – that all good things came from his generous hand. God clearly states, here and elsewhere in Scripture, that he is not interested in fasting for fasting's sake; he is interested in what fasting produces. Fasting is a means to an end, not an end in itself, and that end is a loving community where everyone is included and where God can live among his people.

Mercy, Not Sacrifice

One of the best-known verses on this same subject is found in another of the prophetic books, Micah. The issues are the same. People are ripping each other off using dishonest scales. They are deceitful, lying and violent. Here the prophet asks that most fundamental of questions: what does God really want from us? Does God want us to sacrifice rams or oil? Will God be pleased if I go to the lengths of sacrificing my first-born child? No, no, no! Sacrifice was not instituted by God because he needs us to bow down or, worse still, because he requires the blood of bulls and goats. Sacrifice is there because it should lead us to become people of humility, justice and mercy. These are what God requires of us. Sacrifice is simply a means to an end. So the prophet said, 'He has showed you, O mortal, what is good. And what does the LORD require of you? To act justly and to love mercy and to walk humbly with your God' (Mic. 6:8).

As far as the prophets were concerned justice, mercy and humility were to characterize the relationships people had with each other and with God. Jesus said the same thing when he connected loving our neighbour and loving God. It all makes sense when we understand God's plan to dwell among us while we lovingly relate to each other. That, in fact, is the beautiful picture we find in Zechariah: God coming again to dwell among the people within Jerusalem while young and old alike live lives of fulfilment. As that happened there would be all kinds of repercussions. The appointed feasts once again would become those joyful times when the people celebrated together because things were in order and all people were

included. Then their reputation for joy and happiness would
spread out to the nations around, who would all want a part
of it. They would come and grab hold of the people, wanting
to go with them to Jerusalem because they realized that God
was present and they wanted to be a part of what was going
on. As Jonathan Wilson-Hartgrove puts it, 'Abram's children
will become a people who live together with God in the
world. And when other peoples see how good it is to live
together with their Maker, they will want to come and be part
of God's people too. Through this one people, all the peoples
of the world will be blessed.'[36]

As we sweep through the history of Israel in the Old Testament we cannot but fail to hear the clear call of God for them
to be a community that embodied God's good purposes. It
began with the promise to Abraham but continued through
God's interaction with all the patriarchs, culminating in their
rescue from slavery and establishment within the Promised
Land. The writers of Old Testament history were not hesitant
to continually emphasize that the call to God's people was
given so that all nations could ultimately see what a vibrant,
loving and healthy community was about and be drawn in.
The definition of such a community can be summed up in
one word, and it is to that word we will now turn.

Questions for Community Reflection

1. What might it mean if God was to dwell among your
   neighbourhood and community? Is that a welcome
   and comforting thought or one that fills you with
   some hesitation?

2. Have we in some way also kept the form and lost the spirit? In other words, have we created a version of Christian faith that revolves around either dogma or ritual and at the same time ignored God's desire for justice in our world?

6

God Is on Your Side

'Of all the words which might be used to describe what God wants most for human beings, shalom *seems to be the most appropriate' – Donald Gowan*[37]

A couple of years ago I received an email from Regan, whom I had met in Cincinnati and who had read my first book on the importance of viewing others through the lens of Genesis 1. This is what she said:

'I spent the weekend in Columbus and . . . set up [my stall] at several events, one a fundraiser for Gracehaven, a local aftercare home. A young lady spent some time looking at our things and asked me a lot of questions. Several times as I was answering her, her eyes filled with tears and she seemed very emotional. Eventually she opened up and very awkwardly started sharing some of her story with me . . . She is a survivor of sex trafficking, coming out just four months ago. As we continued to talk, more started spilling out. She had been involved in prostitution for six years, arrested fifteen times, treated like a criminal and not a victim, been raped and beaten and had become addicted to drugs. All of this by the age of 22! But now she is working her way towards freedom.

'I mentioned God casually several times as we talked, and each time she looked down or away, and seemed embarrassed. She then shared about a time when she was horribly beaten and choked and thought she was going to die. The man told her that when he picked her up he had planned to kill her, but had changed his mind because he liked her personality. She said she guessed that God hadn't wanted her to die that night, again looking very awkward about even mentioning God.

'I was pretty broken up, but managed to tell her that he most certainly did *not*, and that *God was on her side*! I wish you could have seen her face. She looked stunned! Her eyes filled with tears and then she just beamed! She had a visible physical reaction to just hearing the message that God was not against her and judging her, but *for* her!'

Isn't it tragic that today so many people believe or feel that God is against them? For the girl mentioned above, this could not be further from the truth, for God is on the side of the poor, the oppressed, all those who have been taken advantage of by their fellow human beings. God's purposes towards us and towards all people reflect blessing, wholeness and life. We see it there in the Garden of Eden, as God makes clothes for Adam and Eve in their nakedness, and throughout the Old Testament as constantly and consistently God communicates his desire that all people live within communities of shalom.

'Shalom' Is a Beautiful Word

'Shalom' is a beautiful word that encompasses so much that is good and positive in life. It's a word worth getting to know.

It makes an appearance in the Hebrew Scriptures no fewer than 210 times, although in our English versions you wouldn't know that because it's translated using different words depending on the context. One of the most common translations renders it 'peace', but peace is only one component of all that shalom means. It's rather like using the word 'meat' to explain food. Food encompasses so many different and rich varieties, of which meat is just one. Similarly, shalom does mean 'peace' but it also means 'well-being', 'wholeness', 'vibrancy', 'joy', 'settledness', 'happiness', 'harmony' and so much else. The word 'shalom' is in fact formed from a verb that is about making something whole or complete.[38] The fact that we have no word in English that exactly translates the concept of shalom might be a reflection of how individualistic our view of the world has become, as well as how segmented our view of life is.

Shalom is a word related in different passages to other key themes in the Bible, such as covenant, salvation, justice and the very nature of God. However, the most profound thing about this word is that it points to a concept that is rooted in community. Wholeness and well-being, which are fundamental to the meaning of shalom in all contexts, are understood within the Hebrew worldview in relation to our neighbour. 'In the vast majority of instances where the word appears, the wholeness of shalom is the wholeness, or completeness, or intactness of a community.'[39]

Shalom Is Freedom in Community

'Shalom' was a common everyday word used within the life of the people of Israel. Donald Gowan, in his study on this word,[40] illustrates its use in the story of Joseph. Once Joseph is seen as favoured by his father and is given the coat of many colours the Bible says that 'his brothers . . . could not speak a kind word to him' (Gen. 37:4), literally, 'his brothers could not speak *shalom* to him'. A few verses later, when Joseph's father sends him off to find out how his brothers are, he says, 'Go and see if all is well with your brothers and with the flocks' (37:14), literally, 'Go and see the *shalom* of your brothers and the *shalom* of the flock.' A few chapters later, when Joseph is in Egypt and the brothers return, having discovered silver in their sacks of grain, Joseph says to them, 'It's all right . . . Don't be afraid' (43:23), literally, '*Shalom* to you; do not be afraid.' Just from these few references it is clear that within everyday language shalom held connotations of well-being, harmonious relationships, good health, safety and security.

The translation of 'shalom' as 'peace' has led to much misunderstanding among those who seek to be followers of Jesus. Some understand peace only as 'the end of hostility between man and God'. We have often been taught that, because of sin, we are alienated from God, but that God is seeking to make 'peace' with us. Interestingly, in the Old Testament, out of the 210 contexts in which the word 'shalom' is found, only one of them can be understood as being about peace between God and humankind (Isa. 27:5).

Others see peace purely as 'the cessation of war'. But 'shalom' is not used to describe 'peacetime'. Rather, the term generally used when Israel had no battles was 'rest', a translation of a different Hebrew word. 'Shalom' was accordingly not used to denote the absence of conflict – a key meaning of the term 'peace' in our language today; the word was far richer than that. 'Shalom is thus a word with a strongly positive content. It is not just the absence of war, of danger, of worry, of fear. It is much more appropriately explained as the presence of prosperity, of health, of happiness, of success.'[41]

Shalom and the Land of Promise

The story of the people of Israel began with the promise to Abram in Genesis 12 – a promise of many descendants and a promise of land, but a promise also involving the blessing of all people. Through the one community, Israel, all communities across the globe were to be blessed.

This is something we should always remember. When people are given a promise by God, or called, or as Paul in some of his writings puts it, 'predestined', it is never for the insular purpose of narrow personal satisfaction; it is always because God wants to bless the whole earth.

As we follow the story through the rest of Genesis and into Exodus, though the focus increasingly moves to the lives of Abraham's descendants, we should not lose sight of the fact that their calling was always to become this model community that had been freed from slavery to live as God intended, and thereby to be a light to everyone else.

The place where they were to be that community of light was Canaan – a land flowing with milk and honey; and the word used to describe what this community would be like is 'shalom'.

Shalom Is God's Assured Covenant and Commitment to People

It is possible to think that 'covenant' has legal implications because of the way it is presently used in western culture, but in Scripture, as Tim Chester says, 'the word "covenant" is a relational term. It signifies a bond of loyalty and commitment, a formally agreed-upon promise'.[42]

The misunderstandings created by translating the word 'shalom' as 'peace' are compounded when looking at covenantal passages. For example, in Ezekiel 37:26 God says, 'I will make a covenant of peace [*shalom*] with them'. This is often thought to mean peace between God and the people. However, when we realize how the term 'shalom' is used we come to understand that the verse is not speaking about God making peace with humankind but rather about God's purpose of fullness, wholeness and completeness being promised to the people of Israel. 'The Covenant form stresses the corporate and social dimension of being related to God. The people of God are a certain type of people; they form a certain type of community which is spelled out by the covenant. This implies strongly that to be in relationship with God is to form a special community which we can call the community of shalom.'[43]

The promise mentioned above from the prophet Ezekiel was given to Israel while they were in exile and it concerned God's plan to bring them back to their land and reunite Judah and Israel. God's twofold purposes, as mentioned already in this book, were again the core message that God was seeking to communicate to them: firstly, his desire that they live full lives characterized by justice, peace and equity, where everyone would be included and would have an opportunity to give and receive; and secondly, that God would be present among them. God said, 'I will put my sanctuary among them for ever. My dwelling-place will be with them; I will be their God, and they will be my people' (Ezek. 37:26,27). The passage goes on to reiterate God's wider purpose: that through this the nations would come and see, and know God for themselves.

Similarly, through the prophet Isaiah God sought to communicate his compassion for the people of Israel and the fact that his purposes for them were good ones. 'Though the mountains be shaken and the hills be removed, yet my unfailing love for you will not be shaken nor my covenant of peace [*shalom*] be removed,' (Isa. 54:10). This covenant was not a peace agreement. It was an expression of God's purposes that Israel would flourish as a community in every area of life. It was an expression of God's desire that Israel would be socially cohesive, that through their work they would be productive, and that they would dwell securely and safely in the land.

This is then repeated in the following chapter of Isaiah, as the prophet extrapolates the implications of God's everlasting covenant with his people: 'You will go out in joy and be led forth in peace [*shalom*]' (Isa. 55:12). This is followed by a reference to a dance of creation as the mountains and hills burst forth in song and the trees clap their hands. The implications clearly extend to the whole created order as the pine trees replace thorn bushes and myrtles replace briers.

Yes, the shalom of God has implications for the entirety of God's created world.

Shalom as God's Blessing on the People

One of the main uses of the term 'shalom' in Hebrew culture was as a greeting, and in that way it was also a blessing. In western culture today greetings have generally become the way we begin a conversation when we meet someone, whereas in the culture of Israel a greeting was taken as the pronouncement of a blessing on the other. When someone greeted another person by saying 'shalom', they were wishing goodness, fullness and wholeness on the other person.

We see this also within the New Testament, as Paul begins each of his letters with a specific greeting, as in Colossians: 'Grace and peace to you from God our Father' (Col. 1:2). Interestingly, the word 'peace' that Paul uses in his greetings is *eirene*, the Greek translation of 'shalom'. For Paul, this was not just a good way to begin a letter; it was the pronouncement of a blessing on the people he was writing to and would have been understood as such by those who received his letters.

Such well-rounded, all-encompassing, positive wholeness denoted within 'shalom' (and *eirene* in the New Testament) was and is God's purpose for his creation. This truth is found in a variety of passages in the Old Testament. The priestly blessing given by God to Moses that was to be pronounced over the Israelites is one example. This blessing would have been spoken twice a day at the time of sacrifice and is one of the most widely used today within the church:

> The LORD bless you
> and keep you;

    the Lord make his face shine on you
        and be gracious to you;
    the Lord turn his face towards you
        and give you peace [*shalom*]. (Num. 6:24–26)

Hebrew writings often used physical imagery and this is no exception, for here we have beautiful pictures of the face of God turning towards his people and radiating warmth and love in the midst of the community. In fact, the Hebrew word translated 'face' could also be translated 'presence', again indicating God's desire to share the life of the community of his people rather than bestow a blessing from afar.

Again, in Leviticus 26, at the end of a series of laws that constitute what is known as the 'holiness code', God says, 'I will grant peace [*shalom*] in the land' (Lev. 26:6). The whole context shows that this shalom is for all Israel, not something for an individual alone. Indeed, even the land is to be touched by this divine shalom, highlighting the fact that the reach of shalom includes the rest of the created order, not just human community. As the people follow God's ways, they will have rain in season, the harvest will be abundant and fruit will be available for all. Shalom is not just for people; it is God's purpose for the whole of the created order, as everything works in the way it was originally designed.

And, as so often in Scripture, the picture is not complete until we understand that God wants to be there, present among the community as they live lives that demonstrate this wholeness, goodness and fullness of life: 'I will put my dwelling-place among you, and I will not abhor you. I will walk among you and be your God, and you will be my people' (Lev. 26:11,12).

As stated above, God's purposes are not simply spiritual or simply about our future. God's desire is that we live lives now of loving, supportive community characterized by the wholeness of shalom while he himself is ever present among us. That was his desire for Israel and that is his desire for us today.

Shalom as God's Purpose within Exile

One of the verses that is often extracted from its context and written in cards or letters as a personal encouragement comes from the prophet Jeremiah: ' "For I know the plans I have for you," declares the LORD, "plans to prosper you and not to harm you, plans to give you hope and a future" ' (Jer. 29:11). There is nothing wrong with such a verse being used as a personal encouragement; of course, God's purposes towards us as individuals are good. However, we must never forget that the original context of this verse had to do with the people of Israel in exile, desperate to get back to the land they believed was core to the covenant God had made with them. It was a prophecy for them as a community rather than an encouragement to an individual. We have a problem in our English translations because we cannot distinguish between 'you' singular and 'you' plural. In this verse, in the original Hebrew it is a collective 'you'.

At the time, some prophets were giving the people a different message; but God told the people to ignore them and to hold on to his promise that he would bring them back. Meanwhile, they were not to sulk, kick their heels or just waste time. Instead, they were to be salt and light within the Babylonian context that they found themselves in. In fact, the word to them was that they should 'seek the peace [*shalom*] and prosperity of the city' (Jer. 29:7). They were also encouraged to pray for the city, because their own prospering would be dependent on the prosperity of the city itself.

We need to stop to realize how completely and utterly radical this was. Their worldview had been rooted in a belief that shalom was for them and not others and was connected to the city of Jerusalem, not to other cities of the world. Now they were told to seek God's good purposes for non-Jews who were living in the midst of what they would consider to be the most pagan and idolatrous of environments. As Alan Roxburgh says, 'Jeremiah's letter suggests that the only way for these exiles to rediscover their identity as God's people is by dwelling in the very place where they imagined God could never be.'[44]

Together with all the other directives God gave about houses, gardens, marriage and so on, it is clear that God didn't want them to think that his purpose of shalom could only be fulfilled back in Jerusalem. Rather, they were to bring that wholeness and fullness of life and plant it in Babylon, a very foreign environment.

This directive of bringing shalom was not something that could be achieved through the efforts of an individual, nor through the exertion of political will; rather, it could only come through the collective efforts of the community, for shalom is a communal concept. As Yoder and Swartley say, 'Right through to contemporary usage one level of meaning has remained important: the Hebrew word Shalom signifies the welfare of persons in community in the most comprehensive meaning of existence.'[45]

God's Purposes for People Are Good

The story of Israel is the story of God's ongoing, life-giving, love-soaked purpose that people would prosper. God is not into constraining people, or preventing them from enjoying life; his desire is that people relate to each other in such mutually supportive ways that everyone finds fulfilment in the deepest part of their being. Such fulfilment is not a specifically spiritual dimension unrelated to the rest of life; rather, it is core to the whole of life. For shalom is not simply a spiritual word: it is also social, intellectual, emotional and physical. It points to well-being in the whole of life because the whole of life is God's domain.

This is the message we need to take out into the world. Instead of trying to beat people over the head by telling them how bad they are so that they realize they need help, we need to lay before them a vision of life in community that reflects the multi-dimensional, integrated and holistic nature of what it means to be human. We need to let people know that God is on their side. We need to explain that God is particularly on the side of the oppressed. We need to share God's ongoing, life-giving, love-soaked purposes for all people.

Questions for Community Reflection

1. How do you react to the idea that shalom is core to God's purposes for all humankind? How is that different from what you have previously imagined God's purposes to be?
2. If shalom does reflect God's purposes and if it is a communal word, what does that mean for us today?

7

The Pivotal Point

'The Word became flesh and blood, and moved into the neighborhood' – John, the disciple of Jesus[46]

Recently, I was invited with a couple of other Oasis staff to spend time with a church that wants to help stop human trafficking. We spoke together about some of the issues and then one of our local staff members shared what had happened to her. You could have heard a pin drop as she talked about the rape and abuse she suffered as an immigrant in a country where she could find no meaningful work. She was driven to the streets and to a life of prostitution out of complete desperation. As we listened, we almost wanted to cry out, 'This is just not fair!'

Eventually she came into contact with our team working in that community and she began the long journey back to health and wholeness. She is now a part of the Oasis community and works to help others who are in the same predicament that she was in. She knows what it is like to be treated in a profoundly unjust way and to be caught in the context of a community where people are left out. She knows what it is like to be in despair – and she also knows what it is like to be rescued. She knows what it is like to be on your own and what it is like to be embraced and accepted.

As the prophet Isaiah began his message to the people of Judah he started on familiar territory. God was fed up with the outward show of religion – their festivals and sacrifices; their offerings and convocations. What he wanted from his people was justice, so that the poorest of the poor who were trapped and required assistance were given the chance to enjoy the prosperity of the community. As ever, God in particular drew attention to the needs of orphans and widows, two groups within the culture of Israel who could not fend for themselves. The early chapters of Isaiah paint a picture that is familiar within the canon of prophetic Scripture: that God's desire and purpose was for people to act justly, love mercy and walk humbly with their God. Instead, though, there appeared to be violence, oppression, exploitation and greed.

The depressing nature of these early chapters is eventually broken with the revelation that a Messiah would come who would bring about this justice and fairness that God wanted for his community and all people. 'For to us a child is born, to us a son is given' (Isa. 9:6) signalled the coming of the Messiah who would establish a kingdom of righteousness and justice.

Within this well-known section of Isaiah is a reference to what the Messiah would be called: 'Wonderful Counsellor, Mighty God, Everlasting Father, Prince of Peace [*shalom*].' Yes, the coming of the Messiah would continue God's agenda for his people and all the peoples of the world to enjoy wholeness, completeness and fullness of life. The prophet continued by saying that there would be no end to the shalom brought about through the reign of the Messiah.

Wow, that was some prophecy!

Justice for All

Throughout the Old Testament there is a deep connection between the emphasis on justice and the coming of shalom. It is injustice that leads to the lack of shalom, and so there was an expectation that when justice was restored in the community of Israel, shalom would be experienced by all.

As the book of Isaiah continues, therefore, another section emphasizes that in the Messiah's coming he would 'bring justice to the nations . . . In faithfulness he will bring forth justice; he will not falter or be discouraged till he establishes justice on earth' (42:1,3,4). This bringing of justice would be seen when the eyes of the blind were opened, captives were freed from prison and those who sat in the darkness of a dungeon were released.

To understand the relationship between these specifics and the issue of justice, we have to realize that if you were blind, you were one of the excluded ones; and the vast majority of those sitting in dungeons were there simply because they were poor. The system meant that the poor were always in debt and debt was the reason the vast majority of people ended up languishing in prison.[47]

These words from Isaiah are therefore not to be understood spiritually; they are literal. Real people suffered because of the unjust systems in their community and it was these injustices that the coming of the Messiah was to change.

Good News to the Shepherds

It is interesting that when the Messiah did come, the first to
hear the news were shepherds: one segment of Israelite society
that at the time formed an excluded group within the wider
community. As shepherds, their constant proximity to animals
meant they were considered unclean and their nomadic lifestyle
meant that their testimony in a court of law was not acceptable. They had little standing in society, held no power, prestige
or importance, and were despised by those who held strictly to
religious etiquette. They were an excluded minority, rather like
the gypsy community in many parts of the world today. Yet
they were the first recipients of the good news that God had
now come in human form to dwell among us.

Perhaps God chose the first revelation to come to shepherds
so that others would not doubt the truth that the good news
was for all people. If it was for shepherds, it must be for everyone else. In fact, in Luke 2:14 the Greek word translated 'those'
in the angels' announcement ('peace to those') is *anthropoi*,
which means the whole of the human race. The angels communicated praise to God and a blessing on all humankind. Guess
what that blessing was? Shalom. The word used here is *eirene*,
which, as we have seen, is the Greek rendering for shalom. It
held all the same connotations of wholeness, completeness and
fullness of life in the context of community.

The Coming of the Prince of Shalom

God became a human being and, as John records, 'made
his dwelling among us' (John 1:14). Incomprehensible to

a waiting world yet glorious in its simplicity and utterly profound in its impact: only God could have dreamt this one up.

This was the extent to which God went to demonstrate that he dearly wants our company, our love, our lives. He wants to dwell among us and be our source of life and hope. As Matthew records, '"they will call him Immanuel" (which means "God with us")' (Matt. 1:23). The God of the universe, who created all we see around us, comes alongside us in our pain and in the struggles of our lives to be with us: that is the truth of the incarnation.

It's the truth of the Bible as a whole, for the coming of Christ into the world is a pivotal point when we grasp that God's purposes are for all people to experience fullness of life, and that this fullness comes when people live in loving, supportive, equitable and just relationships with each other while he is present among them. Yes, God's purposes are all about 'community'.

Jesus coming into the world as God present among humanity was not a new idea or a reversal of what God had been trying to do in the past. In the Old Testament, as we have already seen, God didn't form Israel into a community and then stand at a distance, providing them with some rules and regulations for life. He sought to share their lives, and the tabernacle and then the temple were vehicles for doing that. John certainly saw continuity in the purpose of God, for the word he uses to talk of God '*dwelling* among us' (John 1:14, italics added) is the Greek verbal form for the Hebrew word for tabernacle.

This moment in history is pivotal because, through his life, Jesus showed us who God is and what he is like. It's also pivotal because through his coming to dwell among us we now have a visible representation of God's purposes for the world. And, through the announcement to the shepherds on that Palestinian hillside, it is clear that his coming was not just for the Jews and not just for the religious: his coming was for the whole world, especially for those who had been, up until that point, excluded from his good purposes.

Questions for Community Reflection

1. What difference does it make to realize that Jesus is the Prince of Shalom?
2. How does God's coming to dwell among us speak to you of his desire to live in the midst of our communities?

8

Good Reasons to Party

'God's kingdom is already among you' — Jesus[48]

As a child I spent two weeks every summer in a small seaside town on the Isle of Man. The reason was that my grandfather began a summer outreach programme there in 1901 and my parents continued to lead that when he died.

One of the annual activities that I always looked forward to was the 'Sausage Sizzle'. We would walk a short distance along the coast to a more remote location and there light a fire by the beach and begin cooking our sausages. Served together with buns and ketchup, somehow the food seemed tastier than when dished up on a plate at home. Even the burnt bits that would normally be left at the side of the plate seemed palatable in the wilder and more exposed context of the rocks, sand and sea.

That evening activity was not simply about food, but the food we ate paved the way for building deep relationships, some of which have lasted to this day.

Omitting nearly everything to do with Jesus' upbringing, Scripture jumps from his birth to his appearance as an adult in his late twenties. One of the first steps he took was to invite others to join his community and leave whatever they were doing. It wasn't long before the new rabbi had a core group of disciples who became the backbone of this new community as they travelled hot on the heels of John the Baptist, who had announced that through Jesus a new day was about to dawn.

This new community faced all the struggles that any community would. Some felt left out; some became jealous of their fellow community members; some involved relatives in pressing their claims; one individual eventually turned against the rest. Yet in the midst of this there were times of great joy and laughter as well as times of revelation, as so many of those who followed Jesus slowly realized that he was the one sent by God: the Messiah.

Eating and Drinking

It wasn't long into his three years of itinerant community living that Jesus gained a reputation – or two reputations, to be precise. The first was as a miracle worker: someone who healed the sick and had authority to expel demons. The second was as a person who ate and drank too much – someone who liked to party and did so with the wrong company.

Responding to the particular accusation that he ate too much and drank too much as he feasted with guests at the home of Levi, Jesus made it very clear that 'It is not the healthy who need a doctor, but those who are ill' (Luke 5:31). Tim Chester has written a book on the importance of meals in the life of Jesus and says:

The meals of Jesus . . . represent a new world, a new Kingdom, a new outlook. But they give that new reality substance. Jesus' meals are not just symbols; they're application. They're not just pictures; they're the real thing in miniature. Food is stuff. It's not ideas. It's not theories. It's, well, it's food, and you put it in your mouth, taste it and eat it. And meals are more than food. They're special occasions. They represent friendship, community and welcome.[49]

By eating with those on the edge of society Jesus was signifying that this new world where everyone is included was coming into being.

Associating with people of disrepute was frowned upon. People thought you were doing what God wanted when you refused to eat with those who were 'unclean'. Yet Jesus showed that to eat with the outcast was exactly what God wanted people to do. In fact, he stated this in no uncertain terms to a prominent Pharisee when he was eating in his home: 'When you give a luncheon or dinner, do not invite your friends, your brothers or sisters, your relatives, or your rich neighbours; if you do, they may invite you back and so you will be repaid. But when you give a banquet, invite the poor, the crippled, the lame, the blind, and you will be blessed' (Luke 14:12–14).

I'm not sure we realize how radical these words were and are. Walter Brueggemann, in his short book on shalom, *Living Toward a Vision*, suggests that eating has always reflected how people order their world and points to the way that the civil rights movement in the USA had to stand against separate eating places because the white majority ordered society on the basis of such discrimination. 'Eating is where it's at. There we do our choosing and our shaping of life.'[50] It was for this very reason that Jesus stood against the norms of his cultural context and demonstrated through his meal tables that this coming kingdom was already ordering the world in a different way. Now there were to be no rules except one – love God and your neighbour – and no bars to children or those who were poor participating. All were welcome.

Poverty and Relationships

Poverty always has been fundamentally relational rather than economic.[51] There is an economic dimension to poverty for sure, but at its heart, poverty is about being alienated from other people and having relationships that don't work. By not eating with certain people we are demonstrating their alienation from the mainstream. When people have no say and their voice is not heard it creates deeper wounds in the human spirit than when bread is not readily available. Those considered 'sinners' in Jesus' day were those who were relationally poor: they were not included and their voice was not heard. Jesus gave them a voice and demonstrated the dignity of all people by feasting at their table.

In a western context the significance of whom you eat with is not appreciated. Yet even today in many parts of Asia and the Middle East, when you eat someone's food, in their home, you are seen to be honouring them. That's why Zacchaeus was so bowled over when Jesus announced he was coming to his house (Luke 19:5–6). In western culture, if you say you are coming to someone else's house it can be seen as something of an imposition. When Jesus said that to Zacchaeus, he was honouring him.

Jesus' Final Meal with His Disciples

It is interesting that, as the time for Jesus' death loomed ever closer, he chose the most profound expression of community as the setting for communicating his love for those who had been his closest followers: a meal. And this was no ordinary meal. It was the central meal in the lives of the Jewish people, the Passover. It was a meal celebrating God's rescue of their community from oppression and the subsequent journey to the Promised Land, where God would dwell among them while they would be his people, living in freedom, joy and shalom.

During this meal the bar was raised once again. Instead of being commanded to love their neighbour as they loved themselves, the disciples were now urged to love as Jesus had loved them. That love had just been expressed in the washing of their feet and would very shortly be seen in the giving of his life.

The words of Jesus as he took bread and broke it have become some of the best known in all branches of the church. 'This is my body given for you; do this in remembrance of me' (Luke 22:19). 'Do this' has traditionally been taken to mean the eating of bread carried out throughout the Christian church as part of the service of Communion. Yet these words could also be understood at a deeper level, as several people have pointed out: as an exhortation by Jesus to copy his giving of himself in sacrificial love. I have heard Steve

Chalke say many times that Jesus was inviting his disciples one last time to go the extra mile, to forgive their enemies, to love the stranger – yes, even to give up their lives in sacrificial love.

Dave Andrews in *The Divine Society* makes the same point: that the application of these words is not about holding a regular Communion service; it is about sacrificially giving our lives by living out the agreement (covenant) of love that is characterized by the quality of Jesus' love. In his book he quotes from a letter written by Carlos Christos to his parents from prison, where he had been sent as a result of his work among the poor. In that letter Carlos Christos says, 'Mass is something to be lived rather than attended, and it is to be lived to the extent that we are willing to sacrifice ourselves for the liberation of human beings, and so become God's sacrament in the world.'[52]

The Last Supper was a communal affair that Jesus had eagerly anticipated for some time (Luke 22:15) and at which he was deeply troubled (John 13:21) as the time for his betrayal arrived. It was in this setting again that he urged his disciples to follow what he was about to model for them. Following a rabbi was about learning to do what they did, not simply absorbing the knowledge they shared. And Jesus was about to demonstrate not only the extent of God's love for the world, but also the extent of love that should characterize the community which had been formed around him and which would blossom and flourish once he had gone.

For the disciples this was a profoundly difficult time. They knew something was up but they couldn't quite put their finger on what it was. Following the sharing of the Passover meal

Jesus began talking again about laying down his life, something he had mentioned on a few occasions previously. When Peter questioned him, Jesus predicted his denial. John, in his gospel, then records the longest discourse spoken by Jesus exclusively to his disciples, covering the whole of chapters 14 to 17. The overarching theme of this discourse is the oneness of community.

The Comfort of God's Spirit

Jesus knew the uncertainty and confusion in the hearts of these dear friends of his. The anxiety, I am sure, was palpable as Judas left the room and Jesus asked whether Peter would really lay down his life for him; so he said, 'Do not let your hearts be troubled' (John 14:1). He then went on to both comfort them and exhort them to continue to be the community of faith centred on God and God's purposes for the world. Central to this was the promise that in his leaving they would not become orphans who were bereft of his presence; rather the 'Spirit of truth' would be among them. It is worth noting that Jesus said the Spirit would both invade the space between them as well as dwell within them (14:17). As this happened they would begin to understand the oneness that existed between himself, the Father and them.

This was community. This was God's ultimate purpose.

The quality of these relationships of oneness, Jesus said, was love. In fact, this is repeated twice as he emphasized the relationship between their loving each other and their neighbour (obeying his commands), God loving them, and Jesus' love for them and revelation of himself to them. He then told them not to be worried or concerned, for shalom, his shalom, would be their portion. The word here is again *eirene*, which Jesus then repeated a few moments later (16:33) as he explained that he had said all these things so that this quality of peace, wholeness, completeness and fullness of life would be their portion in the midst of the turmoil that was about to break into their world.

The oneness characterized by love is emphasized again through the image of the branches of a vine (John 15) that gain the required sustenance to bear fruit only through their connection to the vine. As the disciples listened to this it would have been impossible for them to process what Jesus was saying without their historical understanding of Israel as the vine. This was a frequently used picture and would have been the lens through which Jesus' reference to the term was understood. When Jesus said 'I am the true vine' (15:1) he was indicating that God's good purpose to dwell among them as they lived as a community of shalom was now to be fulfilled through him and the new community being formed around him.

Following his words about the sending of the Spirit and the coming persecution, Jesus then brought the discourse to a close with a reminder that they could be a community of shalom because of his overcoming of all that stood against them (16:33). Jesus' eyes were then lifted to heaven as he prayed for what he had talked about to become a reality in their lives (John 17).

Community: A Sign for the World

Jesus, however, was and always had been focused on the world and in his prayer this concern emerged again: 'My prayer is not for them alone. I pray also for those who will believe in me through their message, that all of them may be one, Father, just as you are in me and I am in you. May they also be in us so that the world may believe that you have sent me' (17:20,21). Again, these verses are pointers to a community of people who were living in loving, supportive relationships together and with God at their centre; because of that the circle would be ever-expanding, drawing in others to see, realize and believe that Jesus' way of inclusive love was the only way that God's purposes of shalom for all people could become a reality.

Jesus' prayer that the disciples would be one as a sign to the world only really makes sense when we realize that this was not a homogenous group. The church was to be made up of all kinds of people – Jew and Gentile, rich and poor, slave and free – and the disciples as a group were an example of this. People who would never normally have rubbed shoulders with each other – but rather would have crossed the road to avoid each other – were now brought together in community because Jesus had broken down the walls of hostility between them.

John 17 is not about unity within a group of people who are generally from the same kind of background; it is about profound differences being overcome within the community of God's people. This became the most powerful sign to those outside the church that the way of Jesus was truly the way of fullness of life for all. As Alan Roxburgh says, 'The ways in which the Good News of Jesus brought hope, transformation, and liberation to those cast aside on the garbage heap of the empire, and the ways in which these house church communities so often demonstrated and lived out the reality of a new social order that crossed ethnic and cultural divides could not easily be dismissed.'[53]

Contained within Jesus' prayer for his disciples was a request to the Father for protection. Interestingly, as Gilbert Bilezikian points out, that request was not related to their personal situation or to the fact that they were likely to encounter opposition from other people in the months and years that were to follow. Rather, that prayer for protection was 'to enable them to achieve among themselves the same kind of oneness that prevailed between Father and Son within the Trinity'.[54] Oneness was clearly to be the key definition of the disciples' relationships as the church was born.

The gospels, each in their own way, point us to the formation of a new community that centred on Jesus. There were clearly some disciples who were part of the inner circle and others who formed a wider group who had left their homes and families to live and learn from the rabbi Jesus. The usual tensions that might be expected to emerge within a group that spends extensive time together did so and on several occasions Jesus had to step in and act as peacemaker. Even so, this community not only survived, it thrived. It was built around a new way of understanding the Law and the Prophets that would go on to be foundational once Jesus had returned to his Father. This understanding is highlighted within Jesus' most famous discourse, the Sermon on the Mount, which we will explore next.

Questions for Community Reflection

1. How do you react to the different interpretation given of Jesus' words that form the core of our Communion services? What difference might this make to how we celebrate Communion?

2. How do you feel when you read that God's purpose of oneness is crucial to our being his followers today? What prevents your own community of faith reflecting this oneness?

9

A Revolutionary Take on Things

*'Because our culture is individualistic, we think of righteousness
as the virtue of an individual person. And because our culture
is possessive, we think of it as something an individual possesses.
But righteousness that an individual possesses is self-righteous-
ness. And that is exactly what the gospel says we cannot have'* –
Glen Stassen and David Gushee[55]

Phil, who leads our work in Belgium, was one day chatting
together with some of his team with Supatra, one of the
women who had been trafficked into the country from
Thailand. They were using with her an Oasis resource called
the 'Rhythm of Life' – a tool to help us live reflective lives
built on a holistic understanding of who we are and what we
do. As part of this they asked her what certain symbols meant
to her. It was not difficult for her to appreciate a number of
the symbols, but when it came to the symbol of the mirror, it
made no sense. The mirror is there to help us think through
our identity and image of ourselves as well as our image of
God. Supatra said that she had no self-image. Instead her

identity flowed from her family. In other words, her image was shaped by her closest relationships rather than by her individuality.

That is true for a lot of people who have not been immersed in western culture, and it is far closer to the biblical understanding of personhood than the predominant view in the west.

In his three years of ministry Jesus was intentional about building a community. It included intimate friends, some who were with him most of the time and others whom he saw periodically as he travelled the length and breadth of Palestine. He was the rabbi and they were the disciples; he was the leader and they were his followers.

One day, while in the Galilee area with large crowds around him, he went up a mountainside and was slowly joined by his disciples. The teaching he gave that day includes some of the most famous words he is known to have said. If you were to quote the following sayings to people of different faiths, and even to those with no faith, they would probably know that they came from Jesus:

'Blessed are the poor in spirit.'

'Love your enemies.'

'You are the light of the world.'

'Let your "Yes" be "yes", and your "No", "no".'

'Our Father in heaven, hallowed be your name.'

People were amazed at this teaching then, and they have been ever since. Many who do not call themselves Christians would embrace this teaching as the most profound way for people to live their lives. It's that good.

However, the Sermon on the Mount is not another benchmark of behaviour for people to live up to; 'it's about something that is starting to happen . . . It is gospel: good news, not good advice.'[56] This Sermon on the Mount is really the community sermon. It's all about the new kingdom community that was being launched by Jesus and which was going to be characterized by loving, supportive and just relationships between people who recognized that God was present among them. It's a microcosm of what the Bible is all about.

If You Are Not Doing Well in Life, It's Alright

To appreciate Jesus' opening words, 'Blessed are the poor in spirit' (Matt. 5:3), we have to understand the audience to whom he was speaking. These were ordinary village folk who lived under two main burdens: the occupation of Palestine by the Romans, and the demands of the Jewish religious leaders of their day.

These ordinary folk were fishermen, farm labourers, carpenters, tax collectors and the unemployed. They were those who had a hand-to-mouth existence, with no savings and little opportunity to change their situation for the better. Yet, as we know from experience today, such people often possess deep levels of patience and perseverance and find joy in the ordinary things of life.

These people to whom Jesus was talking were accordingly on the edge and without power or influence; they were in large measure those who were excluded. They were used to living in a context where the strong and powerful appeared to be blessed; but Jesus began his sermon with the words 'Blessed are the poor in spirit, for theirs is the kingdom of heaven'. Wow! That would have got their attention, if the healing miracles hadn't (Matt. 4:24). For years, the message they had heard was about how hard they had to try to keep rules and regulations in order to please God. Yet, however well they thought they might be doing, they always seemed to come up short. Some of them had given up trying. Now this new teacher who had just performed all these amazing miracles was telling them that if they felt they were not making it, they were in a good place. How good was that?

Standing Up for the Rights of Others

At the end of the Beatitudes we run into the thorny issue of persecution (5:10–12). Under the old framework, which interpreted the Bible through the lens of personal salvation from sin, there was a straightforward explanation for this teaching. Persecution would occur because some people would reject the need to repent of their sin and trust in Christ's atoning work. At an individual level we should therefore accept our lot when we are made fun of, are mistreated or even, as in some cases, are violently oppressed.

However, I want to suggest that, as we begin to understand God's purposes for the whole world, these verses take on a whole different meaning. The context, of course, is about meekness, justice, and peacemaking: characteristics of God's deliverance and of the new community being launched through Jesus. What Jesus was communicating was that this new community would be a real contrast to what people had known previously. The Greek word translated 'righteousness' in verse 10 is not connected to personal piety; that is an individualistic reading of the passage. Rather, *dikaiosyne* points to the concept of 'community-restoring justice'[57] and reflects the Old Testament concept of 'righteousness', which meant 'preserving the peace and wholeness of the community'.[58]

This was radical teaching, particularly when Jesus articulated that this community was for everyone, especially for the down-and-outs, prostitutes, lepers and tax collectors. That message would get someone into serious trouble because, if taken on board, a segment of the community would lose out. That segment included those who prospered through ensuring that unjust systems were perpetuated, and it was that group that would be doing the persecuting.

Persecution here is therefore not related to personal piety or holiness. Rather, it is related to standing up for justice and ensuring that all people are included in God's good purposes. How do we know this? Well, Jesus pointed to the persecution of the prophets as being 'in the same way' (5:12), and the prophets were persecuted because they were God's mouthpiece telling the leaders and teachers of Israel that they needed to act justly, not profit from the exclusion and manipulation of those they led.

Together We Are Salt and Light

Following the Beatitudes Jesus told the people that they were the 'light of the world' and the 'salt of the earth' (5:13,14). Both of those metaphors would have immediately found meaning in the minds of his audience because they were familiar images of what Israel was called to be. What is interesting is that these are communal passages, not ones directed at individuals. As noted earlier, modern English translations have lost the differentiation between the 'you' singular and the 'you all' plural, but in these two verses it is the collective 'you all' who are salt and light.

This is therefore not about people being individual lights in the midst of the darkness. It is rather about the new community formed around Christ being a collective witness of the way God intended we all should live. This drastically alters our understanding not only of this passage but also of much of the New Testament, for the vast majority of occasions where 'you' is found it actually means 'you all'. [59]

Seeing the Law from a New Perspective

Just in case the crowds began to think that Jesus' teaching was somehow different from what was contained in the Torah or in the prophetic tradition, he stated unequivocally: 'I have not come to abolish them but to fulfil them' (5:17). Jesus was not against the Law, but he was against the way it was interpreted and used by some of the existing religious leaders. That is clear from the record of many of his encounters with them, Pharisees especially. This was not simply a problem of his time but went back to the time of the prophets themselves.

As we saw earlier, when people live by the form and lose the spirit, life in the community drastically deteriorates. This is what Jesus was pointing out here. When people sought to keep to the letter of the Torah they ended up burdening the very people the Law was there to protect. On many occasions Jesus pointed out that this was the attitude of the religious leaders who imposed strict rules about purity in a legalistic way but failed to have compassion on those who struggled to keep such rules.

An example of this is found in Matthew's own encounter with Jesus, which he records in chapter 9, shortly after the Sermon on the Mount. Jesus was eating with Matthew and other outcasts at Matthew's house when the Pharisees questioned the disciples about what Jesus was doing. Jesus heard this and said, 'It is not the healthy who need a doctor, but those who are ill. But go and learn what this means: "I desire mercy, not sacrifice." For I have not come to call the righteous, but sinners' (9:12, 13). This word that Jesus took from the Old Testament prophet Hosea was, as we saw earlier, exactly the same message the prophets continually told the people of Israel who had failed to be that loving, just, inclusive community that reflected God's purposes for the world. They had carried on with the ritual of sacrifice but had lost what it pointed to: mercy. Form without spirit leads to an emphasis on ritual purity instead of justice and mercy.

For the Benefit of the Whole Community

When Jesus said, 'unless your righteousness surpasses that of the Pharisees and the teachers of the law, you will certainly not enter the kingdom of heaven' (Matt. 5:20), he was not raising the bar higher so that people would have to try harder to keep the Torah and the hundreds of additional pharisaical regulations. Rather, he was saying that this all had to be surpassed by an understanding of the Law as being lovingly and graciously provided by God so that the community could truly live lives of wholeness and fullness of life characterized by shalom.

For example, when the Pharisees complained that the disciples, by picking, rubbing and eating kernels of grain, were not keeping the Sabbath (Mark 2:25–28), Jesus pointed out that the Sabbath wasn't a legalistic framework given to please God; it was a framework that would benefit the community and help them live full and whole lives. In fact, Jesus went so far as to repudiate the legalistic interpretation by saying that even the consecrated bread in the temple was not out of bounds when no other food was available! This shows that Jesus' interpretation of the Law was about unveiling the spirit of generosity, blessing, reconciliation, inclusion and love within its teachings.

Jesus then illustrated this interpretation of the Law that leads to generosity, blessing, reconciliation, inclusion and love, with examples of relational tension, points that were common in the context of community at the time. These included the tension between men and women, fuelled by the tendency of men to divorce their wives with no justification (Matt. 5:31,32). They also included the tension between Roman soldiers and ordinary Jews who could be requisitioned on the spot to assist the former as guides or porters (5:41). More generally, Jesus encouraged those to whom he was talking to make peace in any dispute rather than end up in a court of law (5:25).[60]

Jesus went on to say that in our world of differences, there was no room for exclusion (5:43–47). More than that, when we discover differences between us, and when they begin to create division, we are to proactively seek reconciliation, for we are to love, not hate, and to pray for those who for one reason or another have become our enemies. The point here is that we can all respond well to those who are like us and who are in our group or culture, but real love means reaching out to those who are different.

The concluding verse of this section – 'Be perfect, there-fore, as your heavenly Father is perfect' (5:48) – is one that has been commonly misunderstood, as John Yoder points out:

> Modern concepts of 'perfection' as meaning that which transcends limitations, as being flawless or living up perfectly to every demand of the law, or having a nature devoid of tempta-tion or self-concern, are brought into this text by those who want to use it to prove a point of their own. All such side meanings distract from the simplicity of the gospel demand, which is no more (and no less) than that because God does not discrimi-nate, his disciples are called upon likewise not to discriminate in choosing the objects of their love.[61]

The word translated 'perfect' here really means 'indiscrimi-nate', which makes much more sense in the context. It also makes sense when we understand God's purpose that all people should be included in this new community that will be characterized by loving, supportive relationships.

Throughout this amazing sermon delivered on a Palestin-ian hillside Jesus portrayed a new way of life for those who lived under the enormous burden of daily expectations. That way of life was to be a release from religious observance built on legalism into the abundance and freedom of life that grasped the real underlying reason why the Law had been given: so that all people could flourish and prosper within their community.

Today, many Christ-followers are tempted to order their lives around a new set of expectations that also reflect a legalistic understanding of Scripture. Yet that path is one of form without spirit. It's a dead end. Instead, we must always view Jesus' exhortation here and throughout the gospels within the framework of its true purpose, which is that a community can indeed exist where nobody gets left out.

This famous sermon of Jesus' that contains soundbites that are known around the world is not good advice for individual spirituality. At its heart it is about the reordering of life so that the new community Jesus was launching might reflect God's real purpose for all people.

Questions for Community Reflection

1. What difference does it make if we understand the Beatitudes as a description of where we should stand rather than a benchmark to live up to?
2. How might we appropriate the truth of the Sermon on the Mount if we realize that at its core it is about community living, not individual spirituality?

10

Our 20-Second Prayer

'Jesus brings the biblical tradition to a climax when he defines truth itself as personal rather than conceptual' – Richard Rohr[62]

A few years ago I was visiting the HIV/AIDS centre we had set up near Mumbai for those who had been excluded from their families and communities because of their HIV status. Soon after we arrived we held a community gathering for those living there. That's when I first noticed Madhukshi. She was radiant – warmth and joy flowing from her engaging smile. I wondered whether she was a new member of staff who had recently joined. Then I came to know her story.

Madhukshi's mother had committed suicide because of her husband's alcoholism and other family concerns. This had led Madhukshi into the path of marriage at a young age. She quickly had a daughter and then a son, but both were found to be HIV positive. It was only with the birth of their son that the couple found out that Madhukshi's husband was carrying the virus, as, by that time, was Madhukshi herself.

Madhukshi's son died only a month and a half old; her husband followed a couple of years after. Because her husband's family had not wanted the marriage to go ahead they provided no support. Neither did Madhukshi's own family. She was living in a community where people were very suspicious of HIV and where no one was concerned about her plight. She was on her own.

However, when she knew that she could join the Oasis community near Mumbai she didn't bring any of her possessions with her. Instead, she gave them all away to those in her community – to those who had ignored and shunned her. It was an expression, as was so much else in her life, that she had forgiven them. She was able to move on in her life because she chose not to hold on to the past, however painful it had been. And the fruit of that decision was easy to see in the way she smiled and engaged with those around her.[63]

The Lord's Prayer

Jesus' Sermon on the Mount continues with what is known as 'The Lord's Prayer', which takes about twenty seconds to pray – it is that short and simple. I have prayed it in many different settings. I have prayed it in some magnificent cathedrals as well as in smaller church buildings; I have prayed it in schools and in people's homes. But none of these settings can compare with praying it in the midst of a slum community. It is there that the contrast between the context around you and the words you are uttering gives real meaning to what you are saying. In your midst are those who don't know where their next meal is coming from, as well as those who are heavily burdened in debt to unscrupulous lenders. Forgiveness, deliverance and provision are all urgently required. And when we pray 'your kingdom come, your will be done, on earth as it is in heaven', we cannot either spiritualize those words or pass over them without pondering what it would mean if they were to come to pass.

Just as the Sermon on the Mount is a community sermon, so the Lord's Prayer is a community prayer, and this prayer that Jesus taught his disciples to pray is another instance where the collective 'us' is used and not the individualistic 'me'. 'Give us', 'forgive us', 'lead us', 'deliver us', Jesus said.

Hunger, bitterness, temptation and the battle against evil are not challenges that people should attempt to face on their own. These are community issues and only as people face them collectively can real progress be made.

Forgiveness

For many people there is some confusion when saying the Lord's Prayer because, when it comes to the part about forgiveness, we are never quite sure whether to say 'sins', 'trespasses' or 'debts'. To Jesus' disciples the word 'debt' would immediately bring to mind the numerous references to that word in the Jewish Scriptures. Central among those are the commands in Leviticus 25 in relation to the Jubilee, when all financial debts were to be cancelled.

Jesus said a number of things that related to the year of Jubilee, the most notable of which was in his address in the synagogue at Nazareth, when he clearly articulated his intention to inaugurate a new kind of 'Jubilee'. Jesus said that through himself there would be freedom for prisoners and recovery of sight for the blind (Luke 4:16–21).

It is impossible not to think of the cancellation of debts as part of Jesus' mission statement. The very use of Jubilee language in his debut sermon means that his audience would have thought of it.

Debt, of course, is a profoundly relational issue, not simply an economic one, because it distorts relationships between people. Jesus' mission involved the realigning of relationships so that everyone would be included and could find their place. Debt cancellation is part of this realignment, for where high levels of debt characterize a community, relationships cannot flourish. A wholesome community is one in which people are not indebted to each other.

Immediately following the prayer in Matthew 6 Jesus focused on forgiveness, and his words were totally unambiguous: you can't be forgiven without being a forgiver of others (6:14,15).

Forgiveness gets major airtime on the pages of Scripture. It is a theme that pops up in one guise or another on almost every page as writer after writer in the New Testament points us to its foundational nature for the life of the community of faith.

We must forgive others. We must forgive others from the depths of our being. We must *always* forgive others from the depths of our being, for without doing so we live in self-deception. And that leads to a shrivelling of the soul. When we forgive others, we enter the place of freedom.

This is an example of the narrow way. To forgive is to narrow our focus down to one thing: the release of other people into God's safe hands. When we narrow our focus in such a way it becomes the entrance into expansive freedom, into the place of grace, rest and wholeness. A community that forgives is a community of grace and hope; anyone would want to be a part of it.

Confession

One of the issues caused by the emphasis within the church on victorious Christian living is the fact that it can prevent us from being open about our own brokenness. When we are not able to be vulnerable we lose the power of confession and limit the extent to which we can build intimacy with others.

When James, one of the early apostles, said in his letter to the Christian community, 'confess your sins to each other and pray for each other so that you may be healed' (Jas.5:16), he was complementing what Paul said to the churches about mutuality (e.g. Rom. 12:9–16, especially v. 15). And confession has a power within itself. Talk to anyone who has been part of an Alcoholics Anonymous group and they will tell you. It is essential for the creation of a vibrant community. It is vital for transformation, because transformation comes in some measure through the openness and vulnerability of relationship.

Jean Vanier, who founded the L'Arche communities, reflects on how, in one way or another, we are all addicts:

Some addictions can be seen as destructive, like drink or drugs. Other addictions are less obviously destructive, but they are destructive nonetheless. These can be seen in people who calm their anguish by becoming workaholics or by excessive watching of television, or through possessive relationships or compulsive needs, such as always to be in the forefront and applauded. We can all be addicted to something which is disguised in the clothes of virtue and goodness, but which in reality masks and calms anguish.[64]

There are three things that are essential to our healing. The first is to admit our addictions and our sin, so that we recognize them for what they are. The second is a reordering of our mind to understand God's unconditional love for us. Both of these are commonly taught within the church. The third is the development of a small community that we can trust with our brokenness. Sadly, most churches neither teach this nor provide encouragement for its practice. Such communities of openness, transparency and vulnerability are far more inviting places than those that espouse a culture of victory in all things.

Jean Vanier continues:

> I am struck by how sharing our weakness and difficulties is more nourishing to others than sharing our qualities and successes . . . There is a fundamental tendency to become discouraged in community. We either believe that others are better than we are, or that they don't have to cope with the same problems. This discovery that we are all in the same boat and all have the same fears and weariness can help us to continue. People are nourished by humility, because humility is truth; it is a sign of a presence of God.[65]

The prayer that Jesus taught his disciples to pray contains confession. This is not because we are worthless beings so infected with sin that all we can do is cry out to God for mercy. It is because confession in itself is a part of the healing process. True confession aids transformation rather than simply reminding us of our need of it.

Praying, Giving and Fasting: Tools for Community Living

Jesus' 20-second prayer comes in the middle of a section of the Sermon on the Mount that has three parts to it. One is about prayer; the other two are about fasting and giving. They are all joined together to make a larger point as Jesus encouraged those who followed him to behave differently from the common practice of trying to outdo each other in religiosity. This larger point was that an outward, public and competitive approach to these three disciplines is not what God desires because it does not reflect a heart that is either God-centred or people-centred.

Note that Jesus encouraged his disciples to take a private approach here not because he was trying to create a more personal and individualistic spirituality but because he wanted his disciples' motivations to be fundamentally those that served God and others. They were not to desire personal prestige. Jesus encouraged them to 'go into your room' (Matt. 6:6), not as an escape from community responsibility but because of it. Praying, giving and fasting are all tools to build a healthy community, one in which God can dwell.

Prioritizing Love and Justice

Following that, Jesus then addressed issues of envy, greed and compromise, and the need for his followers to be whole-hearted in their discipleship. He spoke about the freedom they would find as they followed him and told them that they did not have to worry about those things in life that often become sources of anxiety. Instead they could reorientate their lives around the priorities of his kingdom.

Jesus' injunction to 'seek first his kingdom and his righteousness' (6:33) is not a command to greater personal evangelism or personal piety. Rather, in keeping with the whole of this sermon, it is about prioritizing the love and justice which are hallmarks of this new era which was then being inaugurated: this new community of followers who would seek to do to others what they would want done to them. That, as I mentioned earlier, is the narrow path that leads to life; for the easy path is the selfish one, the greedy one, the path of personal prestige and fulfilment.

The Rock and the Sand

As Jesus neared the end of his discourse he issued a warning. Some people who thought they represented God because they prophesied, cast out demons and performed miracles would be in for a shock because even though they had used God's name, they had not done what God desired. They had misunderstood God's intentions. Those intentions had been made clear by Jesus right here: they were about doing to others what you would want done to you; about forgiveness, mercy and love. This was the narrow path, the route into the expansive place of God's kingdom, the community he was ushering in and which, indeed, was already among them.

You see, it is possible to prophesy, cast out demons and perform miracles and not be a good neighbour or work for the benefit of the whole community, seeking shalom for all. This is the point. The sermon is about a reordering of priorities around what God really desires. Those listening to these words at that time would undoubtedly have had in their minds the legalism of the religious leaders of their day which appeared to be what God wanted but actually wasn't. It was form without spirit.

This sermon – which is so focused on how people in Jesus' new kingdom community will fulfil all the Law and the Prophets – is then drawn to a close with a simple contrast between two house builders: one building his house on the rock, the other building it on the sand (7:24–27). The contrast could not be clearer.

It's a contrast between those who live lives of justice, reconciliation, forgiveness, inclusion, generosity and love with those who are greedy, violent, proud, vengeful, and consumerist. It is about real actions not just belief. It's about putting what has been heard into practice, not letting it in through one ear and out through the other. It's about how we live in community together, not about individualized spirituality.

Following the teaching of Jesus is not simply about obeying him; it's about joining with others who are also following his teaching. To understand the Sermon on the Mount we have to understand it as Jesus' community sermon.

Questions for Community Reflection

1. Are you part of a confessional community in which transparency is encouraged? If not, what would it take for groups you are involved with to become like that?
2. Where are the challenges in our lives collectively between form and spirit and between legalism and freedom?

11

The Real Thing

'The gospel is about us before it is about me' – Scott McKnight[66]

One of the most amazing days of my life occurred in 2012 when back in Mumbai. Our staff there had organized a reunion of those who had been helped through our work over the previous twenty-year period. They had sent information about the event via word of mouth so they had no idea how many would turn up. The hope was that at least fifty people would come. When I arrived there were already 120 there. Former street children shared how they were now working in call centres; HIV-positive women were now married with children; and some who had been on the verge of despair were now fully integrated within a loving, supportive community.

As they spoke about what God had done in their lives they included work, faith, health, relationships, hope and many other aspects that make our lives what they are. Truly the gospel in all its forms had been preached, accepted and lived out.

John, the Forerunner of Jesus

Having looked at Jesus' teaching about the characteristics of a God-centred, vibrant and healthy community, we now focus in on Jesus' central message: his gospel. Of course, Jesus began his declaration and explanation of this on the back of John the Baptist, who came 'preaching a baptism of repentance for the forgiveness of sins' (Luke 3:3). The context Luke provides for this is taken from Isaiah 40, which he quotes (vv. 4–6). Today, if someone told you that 'a baptism of repentance for the forgiveness of sins' was the topic of the sermon at a church service, what would you think would be the content? Most likely you would expect a call to avoid a long list of personal sins prevalent in our society today. What is interesting here is that when the crowds asked John what they should do (3:10), he did not focus on personal holiness but rather on communal justice. Those who had two of something should give one away; those who had food should share it with those who didn't. The tax collectors were to act justly in the taking of taxes, and soldiers were not to extort money or accuse people falsely (vv. 11–14).

This all seemed to ring true for the people because they wondered whether John was actually the Messiah himself. John explained that he was not but that the Messiah was on his way. Luke then tells us that 'with many other words John exhorted the people and proclaimed the good news to them' (v. 18). In John's eyes the gospel was connected to God's purpose to create a community that works for all. 'The good news of John was the good news of shalom justice.'[67]

So when John said 'repent', he was not wagging his finger at people telling them that they were in danger of eternal damnation. Rather he was extending his arms in invitation so that they could change the way they lived and embrace the outcast, stranger and those in need. Countless prophets had made a similar invitation over the centuries. As God's mouthpiece, the prophets had urged God's people to live just, peaceful and inclusive lives.

The fearful picture many evangelicals have in their minds when they hear the word 'repent' doesn't make sense in the context of what is recorded by Matthew, Mark, Luke and John. When it sits alongside the term 'gospel' it is much more helpfully understood as an invitation to enter the abundant life that we have already seen as characteristic of God's purpose for people in the Old Testament. In essence 'repent' means to turn around and follow a new path and a different agenda. It's a word that seeks to draw people in, not force them into a corner.

The Multifaceted Nature of the Gospel

As you probably know, the word 'gospel' is the Greek for 'good news'. Yet you wouldn't think that by the way the term 'gospel' has been used by many people in recent years and is still used today. In fact, because 'gospel' has become the generic term for only one aspect of good news, it has been hijacked to the detriment of us all.

Mark opens his record of Jesus' life, death and resurrection with the words 'The beginning of the good news about Jesus the Messiah, the Son of God' (1:1). This use of 'good news' was consistent with other writings in the Roman world. In fact, almost the same words are used in a decree about Augustus, who 'began for the world the good news that happened because of him' (from *The Son of God in the Roman World* by Michael Peppard [OUP, 2012]).[68] The word 'gospel' was often related to the beginning of a new era and to the coming of peace. Mark talked about 'the beginning of the good news' because the gospel was not thought of as a one-off event but as the start of a period of time that was to increasingly bring about what everyone desired.

This use of the term 'good news' in general life is consistent with its use within the canon of the Bible. A cursory reading in any concordance will show you that 'gospel' is used for a number of different things all related to Christ. If we want to define the good news we cannot simply take one of these; we have to take them all. So when someone today asks, 'Do you preach the gospel?', the answer is, 'Which gospel are you referring to?' Sadly, the gospel has been reduced to the good news of personal salvation: that I am forgiven of my sins and enter a relationship with God that will culminate in my going to heaven. This is indeed good news, but there's a lot more good news besides.

Jesus' Use of the Term 'Gospel'

When Jesus began his public life he stood up in the synagogue in Nazareth and was handed the scroll of the prophet Isaiah to read. He could have chosen any passage. Instead of some of the better-known passages about the coming of the Messiah he chose one about the gospel for the poor, the blind,

the captives and the oppressed and read from that (Luke
4:18,19). The gospel here is about freedom, recovery, release
and favour. It's about those who are on the edge of society
being welcomed into the new community, the kingdom that
Jesus was inaugurating. It's about having the chance to start
again. It's about inclusion.

Inclusion is the gospel, or a key part of it. The good news
is not simply for those who are excluded; it is the truth that
the excluded are now included within God's purposes for the
world. Jesus didn't need to wait long to discover that the gospel
that the excluded were now included would not be welcomed
by all. Initially amazed by the gracious words that Jesus spoke
(v. 22), the people soon became upset with him to the extent that
they tried to kill him (v. 29). The reason was that in anticipating
his rejection by those in the town he grew up in, he gave two
examples from the Old Testament of God's engagement with
Gentiles: Naaman, and the widow of Zarephath. For the Jewish
people, the Gentiles were outside God's good purposes, so for
Jesus to include them provoked a ferocious reaction.

The Good News of the Kingdom

As Jesus wandered the length and breadth of Palestine over
the subsequent three years the most common term he used
when talking about good news was 'the kingdom'. In fact,
'the kingdom' was so central to Jesus' teaching that it more
than anything else is the topic of the parables. Whatever we
may think about the term 'kingdom', to understand what
Jesus was saying we have to understand what it would have
meant in the minds of those who heard Jesus speak.

'Kingdom' was a term used by Jewish rabbis of the day to indicate those who obeyed the Law. In fact, obedience to the Law was so important to the Pharisees because they believed that if all Jews obeyed what it commanded for a single day, God would come and usher in his kingdom on earth in completeness. So every Jew who obeyed the Law was bringing about the kingdom, even though not in its fullness. It was anticipated that one day it would come in its fullness, and it was for that day that the Jews all hoped. On that day the Jewish people would be liberated and God's reign would be supreme throughout the world.

As Jesus used the terms 'kingdom of God' and 'kingdom of heaven' (which are synonymous) he deviated from the usual rabbinic teaching by saying that this kingdom was for the poor in spirit, for those who mourned and were meek and who longed for justice and mercy. He was not suggesting that the Torah was unimportant; rather he gave the Law its fullest meaning: the law of love. So when he said, 'unless your righteousness surpasses that of the Pharisees and the teachers of the law, you will certainly not enter the kingdom of heaven' (Matt. 5:20), he was not saying that we need to try harder to obey the Torah. Rather, he was saying that God's kingdom is really about a loving, supportive, forgiving community where everyone is included and where people truly do love their neighbour as they love themselves.

Paul's Take on the Gospel

As we move on to look at the term 'gospel' in Paul's writings we discover that he used it in a number of different ways.

On some occasions he refers to the gospel as the 'gospel of God', the 'gospel of his Son' or the 'gospel of Christ'. On these occasions he talks about the central importance of faith and grace and the fact that, through Jesus, death has been defeated and sin overcome. But Paul also talks about the gospel meaning that, through Christ, Gentiles and Jews are united together within the family of God: this new, loving, supportive community that is to demonstrate how everything that keeps people apart from each other has been dealt with.

This must have been what he also had in mind in his letter to the Ephesians as he talked about the 'gospel of peace' (Eph. 6:15). Again, the Greek word used here is *eirene*, which encompasses the wholeness, completeness and fullness of life that was always God's purpose for all people. 'Paul's understanding of community is nothing less than the gospel itself in corporate form!'[69]

The Community at Colossae

In his letter to the church at Colossae Paul begins with some beautiful words of encouragement, telling them that, having heard of their faith and love, he constantly thanks God for them. In Colossians 1:4,5 'faith' in Christ and 'love' for others in the community are seen as integral. It's as if it is unthinkable that someone could have one without the other, for they both spring from the same place: hope. They have heard about this hope because it is part of the gospel. In the next few paragraphs the word 'gospel' is found four times and the word 'kingdom' twice as Paul goes back and forth between talking about Christ and talking about the community of which they are a part.

In the section from 1:15–20 it is widely thought that Paul quotes from one of the hymns of the early church that focuses on the comprehensive nature of Christ's engagement in creating, sustaining and reconciling the entirety of the cosmos. It is interesting that again Paul chose the word *eirene* in verse 20 to sum up the results of Christ's death. 'This hymn is thus a truly comprehensive statement about peace on earth. It deals not only with the reconciliation of human beings to God and one another, but also with God's intention to bring peace to the whole world of nature as well.'[70] This whole section of the letter illustrates how, for Paul, the gospel had implications at individual, communal and cosmic levels.

This letter to the community at Colossae just does not make sense if one tries to read it through an individualistic lens. Fundamentally, the implications of what Paul is saying in the first part of the letter about the gospel and about the kingdom are extrapolated into the specifics of how the Colossian community of faith is to live. At its heart, that comes down to relationships.

As with his letters to other churches such as at Ephesus and Rome, ultimately Paul was not interested in his readers gaining an understanding of conceptual truth: he was interested in them being the image of God to the world. And he knew that the only way to do that was by modelling a different kind of community from the one that had been created around them. In fact, as Brian Walsh and Sylvia Keesmat so eloquently show in their wonderful commentary on Colossians, Paul's letter only makes sense when it is read in the light of the Roman Empire that supposedly offered peace, prosperity and fruitfulness. In reflecting on Colossians 1:15–20 they say:

> In a world populated by images of Caesar, who is taken to be the son of God, a world in which the emperor's preeminence over all things is bolstered by political structures and institutions, an empire that views Rome as the head of the body politic in which an imperial peace is imposed – sometimes through the capital punishment of crucifixion – this poem is nothing less than treasonous. In the space of a short, well-crafted, three-stanza poem, Paul subverts every major claim of the empire, turning them on their heads, and proclaims Christ to be the Creator, Redeemer and Lord of all of creation, including the empire.[71]

The Empire and the Kingdom of God

The contrast between the empire of Rome and the kingdom of God could not be starker. The former demanded allegiance and kept people in fear through threats of punishment and promises of the good life that never materialized for the vast majority. The kingdom of God, on the other hand, was built on willing allegiance prompted by love and promised shalom in an inclusive way for all. In short, this was a contrast between violent marginalization and redemptive inclusion.[72]

Throughout this letter Paul was communicating to the community at Colossae that all they required for modelling 'redemptive inclusion' was theirs through Christ. The 'powers and authorities' had been overcome (2:15); their 'earthly nature' (3:5) had no hold because they were 'hidden with

Christ' (3:3); and the old barriers of Jew and Greek, circumcised and uncircumcised, slave and free, were no longer relevant (3:11). It was now possible for them to 'Let the peace [*shalom*] of Christ rule in [their] hearts, since as members of one body [they] were called to peace [*shalom*]' (3:15).

What is the contrast between God's kingdom and the empires of this world today? Traditionally, people have taken the difference to be that between a physical and a spiritual kingdom, but that is built on a false understanding of what Jesus came to accomplish. If we go back to the Sermon on the Mount we have to conclude that the difference is rather that between revenge and peace, hate and forgiveness, personal prestige and real generosity, exclusion and inclusion. These are the real differences that are to be modelled in the church as a sign that the kingdom is truly among us.

Gospel, Kingdom and Community

The gospel according to Jesus and the gospel according to Paul are both about the establishment of a kingdom that stands in contrast to the kingdoms of this world. That kingdom finds expression as communities of people who were once enemies and who once stood opposed to each other but are now reconciled and practise the law of love. In doing that and in being the 'body of Christ' they demonstrate to the world God's purposes for all humanity as well as for the entirety of creation.

The terms 'gospel', 'kingdom' and 'community' cannot be separated from each other; they are interrelated. The gospel is the gospel of the kingdom, and the kingdom finds expression through the new community of faith, inaugurated through Jesus' life, death and resurrection, whereby people once alienated from each other and from God are now drawn into relationships that reflect God's purposes of shalom for the whole earth. As Scott McKnight puts it, 'We confess that the gospel is the work of God to restore us in the context of a community to God and to others for the good of others and the world.'[73]

For Our Day

Somehow we have to recapture for our day this fuller understanding of the good news, for the narrow definition that has been adopted within the evangelical church has caused a lot of damage and, in my view, led to a lot of unnecessary debate about issues that would not otherwise have arisen.

An individualistic approach to life has led to an individualistic reading of the Scriptures, out of which a version of the good news has become the norm that in truth embraces only an individual response to a very personalized message.

With that mono-dimensional understanding of the gospel, everything else which is seen as separate from the gospel and secondary to it is then considered to be an add-on. So it may be good for Christians to be concerned for the poor or to get involved in issues of justice, but these activities are then perceived either to be opportunities to share the narrow individualized gospel or simply to be good activities in themselves. They are not seen as inherently a part of the gospel itself. This leads to a separation between a saving gospel (preaching good news with a view to personal response) and a social gospel (being good news with a view to community transformation). This separation is not true to the original vision of Messiah Jesus and is yet another example of the tragic and unbiblical tendency to separate the spiritual and the physical, the sacred and the secular.

Taking short sections out of what is written in the New Testament – particularly out of some of Paul's letters – and then appropriating them for an individual constructs this mono-dimensional view of the gospel. But this involves extracting passages from their contexts and ignoring most of the Old Testament.

The Multi-Dimensional Gospel and the Testaments

On the other hand, not only does a multi-dimensional understanding of the gospel help us take cognizance of the whole of Scripture, but it also provides much greater coherence between the Old and New Testaments. If our faith is built around personal salvation, we have to address the huge disconnect between the two. The Old Testament has very little to say about a salvation that is concerned with just the spiritual side of our lives or our final future. It has everything to say about salvation and the present predicament of slavery, oppression and injustice within the context of the Israelite community.

It seems to me that, if we make personal salvation the key interpretative lens of the New Testament, we have to conclude that God has completely changed the goal posts between the Old and the New Testaments. If, however, we embrace the multi-dimensional nature of the gospel, we can see real continuity between God's dealings with people prior to the coming of the Messiah and what happened following Jesus' life, death and resurrection.

I believe that the multi-dimensional good news is the real thing.

Questions for Community Reflection

1. What misunderstanding has been caused by people using the term 'gospel' to mean only one aspect of the multifaceted good news?
2. If community and kingdom are inseparable from the gospel, what are the implications for us as the church today?
3. How has an understanding that the kingdom is purely spiritual caused us to disengage from the realm of community engagement?

12

What's Mine Is Yours

'Wherever Christians are in relationship there is the body of Christ in its entirety' – Robert Banks[74]

A couple of years ago I was visiting the community centre we run in the midst of a slum in Bangalore in southern India. While I was there one of the mothers of a child in our pre-school came in overjoyed. I wondered why. One of our staff there explained that she had had difficulties finding the money to keep another of her children in school as she could not afford the fees. When this fact became known by others who attended a group that met in this centre, everybody chipped in. That included the cleaner. Because of their generosity she had enough money to send her child to school.

Early Days in the Community of Faith

The period after Jesus rose from the dead began with forty days when the disciples had intermittent interaction with Jesus. The focus of his input to them was interestingly a continuation of all he had said before about the kingdom of God. There is evidence that their grasp of this was somewhat faulty because they still saw the kingdom much more in terms of Israel's future liberation, which is why they asked whether now was the time this was going to occur (Acts 1:6). However, once the Holy Spirit had been given in Acts 2, this small group grew in both understanding and numbers. In fact, it quickly became a vibrant and intentional community.

Before this first community was formed on the Day of Pentecost, Peter brought his proclamation of the good news to a conclusion with an affirmation that Jesus was both Messiah and Lord. Jesus was the one to usher in the new era of shalom that the Jews had long waited for but he was also, in contrast to Caesar, truly to be worshipped. Those listening were 'cut to the heart' (2:37) and asked what they should do. Peter's response was that they should turn their lives around to live differently – the meaning of 'repent' – and that they should be baptized in Christ's name as an indication of this turnaround and the forgiveness of their sins. Peter seemed not just to preach but to plead with them, and the result was an overwhelming response, with 3,000 people impacted. His message of 'salvation' concerned the present and the very practicalities of life as he exhorted them to 'Save yourselves from this corrupt generation' (2:40).

Thereafter, in Luke's record of events there is evidence of an extraordinary quality of community among the growing number of disciples. This was characterized, among other things, by generous sharing. Such sharing was not an occasional practice that stood out from the norm, but rather became characteristic of the way people related to each other.

Everything in Common

Luke's narrative of what happened as a result of the 'conversion' of these 3,000 people must not be overlooked. Some commentators have focused on the fact that miraculous signs were a regular occurrence; others have focused on the fact that they met for teaching and prayer. But the greatest change in their lives was that they were now part of a vibrant, supportive, inclusive, just and loving community, and all who were part of this community constantly celebrated by sharing meals in each other's homes. More than that, they 'had everything in common' (2:44) and ensured that the needs of others were taken care of by community members selling their possessions and giving the proceeds away. As a result, there were no needy people among them (4:34).

'Having everything in common' must have become a key quality of the community of faith. The disciples were not responding to a new idea here; they were simply continuing what they had learnt over three years of community living with Jesus. It's clear from the gospel records that Jesus' small community did live communally, pooling their resources or what was given to them by others and then distributing them beyond the group as well as using them for their own needs. Judas had been tasked with looking after their common purse. John Howard Yoder says that the pooling of resources was the natural outworking of those in the early church constantly and consistently eating together. 'It arose not as the fruit of speculation or discussion about ideal economic relations; it was not something added to what was already going on. The sharing was rather the normal, organic extension from table fellowship.'[75]

It is important that we grasp the revolutionary change here. The description of them being 'one in heart and mind' (4:32) demonstrates how the gospel had its most profound effect at a communal level. It is clear that their understanding of Christ's death and resurrection was not simply something to be personally appropriated. Rather, Christ's death and resurrection inaugurated a new era in which his people lived in inclusive relationships in fulfilment of the law of love, all the time aware of his ongoing presence among them. The picture of what God had desired Israel to be, for the sake of the whole world, was now finally coming true. It must have been exciting to be a part of that.

Issues of Justice

As this Jerusalem-based community grew, practical issues began to arise, most notably the fact that one group of widows was being overlooked when it came to ensuring all had enough to eat (6:1). The disciples' response was to ensure that a justice committee[76] was established made up of the godliest and wisest people. The issue was that important for, above all else, their expression of community was not merely a by-product of personal faith but rather the central witness that Jesus' death and resurrection had inaugurated a new, all-inclusive society.

Baptism

As the Jesus movement continued to grow, baptism became the rite of initiation as both individuals and households joined this community. Peter encouraged this in his first sermon on the Day of Pentecost (2:38). Everyone who responded to his gospel message was accordingly baptized in the *mikveh* pools outside the temple. Thereafter, baptisms occur on many occasions through the book of Acts.

Baptism signalled turning away from a previous way of life that was fundamentally about injustice, oppression of the weak, hostility towards enemies and so on. When Peter said 'Repent and be baptised, every one of you, in the name of Jesus Christ for the forgiveness of your sins', those listening would not have turned their attention to a mental list of personal moral failings. Rather, their attention would have gone to their failure as a people to live as God intended as well as their failure to recognize Jesus as the Messiah who was to bring the fulfilment of God's promises to Israel. Not only had they not recognized him, but they had also been complicit in his crucifixion.

Baptism was not primarily one person's declaration that they had sinned and needed to be forgiven – which is what it has become today. Rather, it was an initiation into a community of people who stood against the ways of the world through their inclusivity and love. The world perpetuated the divisions between Jew and Gentile, slave and free, men and women, rich and poor. Within the community of Christ-followers, that was no longer the case. 'Thus the primary narrative of baptism is the new society it creates, by inducting all kinds of people into the same people. The church is (according to the apostolic witness – not much of its later history) that new society; it is therefore also the model for the world's moving in the same direction.'[77] In baptism 'the natural kinship structure into which the person

has been born and which previously defined his place and
connections with the society is here supplanted by a new set
of relationships'.[78] This was an enormous change in a culture
where identity and prestige were based on social standing.

On a number of occasions the New Testament mentions
that whole households were baptized. This would be very
strange if baptism were primarily focused on the individual's recognition of their personal moral failure. On the
other hand, if households operated as micro-communi-
ties, and those who led them had authority over servants,
slaves, children and others within an extended family, it
makes more sense. Baptism signalled the end of one way
of experiencing community and an initiation into a whole
new community – reordered according to the values of the
kingdom of God.

As a household made up of young and old, men and
women, slave and free stepped forward to be baptized, they
were declaring that their social relationships were no longer
to be dictated by their culture. Instead, their oneness as the
community of Christ meant that love, equality and justice
were to be the marks of how they treated each other. This
can't have been straightforward. Indeed, the fact that many
problems occurred in the redefining of these relationships
is evidenced by the fact that Paul addressed this topic in so
many of his letters.

Household of Faith

One of the metaphors or models Paul used to describe the
church was 'household of faith'. That seems an odd phrase

until we realize that 'household' did not refer to a nuclear family of four or so individuals, as it would for us in the west today.[79] Instead, 'household' was an extended grouping together of several generations with servants and others who would all have lived together. In other words, it was a micro-cosm of community.

The household (*oikos* in Greek) would not only have been the place where people lived but would also have been an economic unit where work was done and in which people founded their identity. In most households there would have been space allocated for travellers and visitors, as journeys were long and people needed a place to stay and find refreshment. So when Jesus sent out the disciples to the towns and villages he was about to travel to, he told them to join that micro-community and enter fully into all its activities, including whatever work was done there. Whenever they arrived at someone's *oikos* they were to offer the blessing of shalom and then accept the hospitality offered rather than look around for a better offer (Luke 10).

The term 'household' is used in several of Paul's letters, including that to the church in Ephesus, where he reminded this predominantly Gentile community that although they were once foreigners, they had now become citizens within God's people. This meant being a part of God's household.

Some of the other terms Paul used are 'building', 'man', 'temple' and 'dwelling'. As we have already seen, the term 'dwelling' was used of the coming of Jesus into the world; now it was used of the Spirit of Christ within the community of the church. For some reason the emphasis on the Holy Spirit's presence within Christians individually has shielded us from the more important truth, given greater emphasis within Scripture, of the Spirit's presence among us collectively. As Robert Banks says, 'Union in the Spirit involved union with one another, for the Spirit was primarily a shared, not individual, experience. The gospel is not a purely personal matter. It has a social dimension. It is a communal affair. To embrace the gospel, then, is to enter into community. A person cannot have one without the other.'[80]

Fellowship

As Luke recorded those early days when the church began to be established in Jerusalem he mentioned four dynamics that were part of this new community: teaching, prayer, eating together and fellowship. These had been the four pillars of the community focused around Jesus. It is no surprise therefore to find them in the earliest Christian community in Jerusalem.

Let's focus on 'fellowship'. This word originally covered a range of activities that were concerned with mutual support, encouragement and practical assistance. The Greek word translated 'fellowship' is *koinonia*, which was a business term in vogue at the time signifying a partnership or joint venture. Within the Christian community this word came to mean the spirit of generous sharing that was a hallmark of the early church.

In Luke's record of the earliest days of the church in Jerusalem he describes fellowship not simply as an activity but as a definition of the church. In Acts 2:42 he says they devoted themselves to 'fellowship'. Fellowship was expressed in the common meal, in the distribution of resources to those in need and in a multitude of other ways.

It's clear from many of Paul's letters to churches beyond Jerusalem that fellowship was central. Robert Banks suggests that, in Paul's eyes, 'fellowship' was core to the community life of the early followers of Jesus. In looking at what marked out Christian fellowship from other forms of fellowship, Banks stresses that relationships were the identity marker of Christian community. He writes, 'The focal point of reference for Paul's communities is neither a book nor a rite, neither a code nor a cult, but a set of relationships.'[81]

Loving Relationships

Paul certainly talks a lot about relationships in his letters. Towards the end of his letter to the Corinthian church he flows into what is probably his most widely read discourse on love (1 Cor. 13). His encouragement to 'Follow the way of love' (14:1) reflects the words of Jesus on many occasions to his disciples that loving your neighbour was the fulfilment of the Law. Love, of course, has no meaning outside of relationship and for Paul, when a Christian community begins to live in love, it is both an expression of God's purpose that communities of shalom should be established and a means of creating and strengthening them.

Furthermore, Paul's letters are full of loving concern for those to whom he wrote. He frequently used terms of endearment like 'beloved', or 'brothers and sisters'. He consistently expressed gratitude for those in each of the cities to which he was writing and reminded them of his prayers for them.

Often Paul mentioned individuals by name and he was always warm in his greetings. Paul not only spoke about the way of love, he modelled it, often while in circumstances that were full of personal hardship.

The Body of Christ

Just before his great discourse on love in 1 Corinthians 13 Paul emphasized the nature of oneness that the church has because of the Spirit. This is important when people are gifted in different ways and inspired and equipped differently by God through his Spirit. All this is so that the community can function effectively and everyone play their part. The term Paul used here is one that was clearly a favourite: the 'body of Christ'. His point here was that everyone belongs; everyone has a part to play; everyone's joys and burdens are shared with each other in equal measure.

I am not sure that there is a clearer analogy that could be used to illustrate God's purpose of creating a just, equitable, supportive community.[82] The body was an ancient way to describe a human community. Paul didn't say that this was something to be worked towards; rather, he constantly used language that reflected a belief that this was definitive of the church as it was.

In the context of the household churches that Paul was writing to, this was revolutionary because it spoke of the irrelevance of social, political and economic status. All those things were to be left on the garbage heap, as Paul stated in a personal note in his letter to the Philippian church community (Phil. 3:7–9). For Paul, the church was never meant to become institutional or hierarchical. It was always meant to be a body of people with Christ as Lord, Christ at the centre, characterized by relationships based on love which subverted the world's relationships based on power.

The Radical Call to Community

It is impossible to read the early chapters of the book of Acts and not recognize that the most profound definition of the church was that of community. This community of Christ-followers stood out from its surrounding culture in two distinct ways. The first was the nature of relationships in which all boundaries were broken down. The second was the remarkable way in which all members of the community were catered for.

We can deduce from this that, for these early disciples, the way of Jesus meant the way of inclusion, justice and equity – principles that were core within Jesus' teaching, central to the gospel, and also core within Paul's definition of community.

This poses huge challenges for us today. How do we become a community that is characterized by the quality of oneness that was evidenced in the early church? How can we become sharers to the extent that needy people don't exist? How can we become known for justice? How can we exude such 'fellowship' that our reputation is one of complete and utter commitment to each other?

Sadly, although this may be true in some church communities, we have bought into the individualistic and consumerist culture of our times to such an extent that in most churches our relationships are seldom a reflection of the multifaceted gospel. We carve out time to attend services and meetings as well as run the important activities of our congregations, yet we can remain blissfully unchanged in the quality of our relationships.

Jesus said, 'This is how everyone will recognize that you are my disciples – when they see the love you have for each other' (John 13:35).[83] From their emphasis on mutual love, the disciples clearly believed that to be true.

If people in your church were asked what a Christian was, how many would provide you with a description of community rather than a statement of belief? God's overarching purpose for humanity is that we live in loving, supportive relationships while he lives present among us. God is not only interested in my personal walk with him; he also wants to invade the space that exists between me and others in my community. He wants the oneness that is now part of our identity as the body of Christ to be worked out in our relationships. He wants to participate in our lives – carrying our burdens as well as sharing our joy and laughter in times of celebration.

> The Church is not a random collection of individuals who happen each to believe in Jesus Christ, who happen to be working out 'their own salvation', who happen to be living in proximity to one another, who happen to enjoy the same preachers and musicians and liturgy, and who happen to affirm the same doctrinal convictions. The Church is a community of faith wherein humans are 're-commissioned' to one another.[84]

Building grace-filled forgiving communities is a huge challenge in a consumerist and individualistic culture. Both consumerism and individualism numb us to the plight of other people. They enable us to stay a safe distance and to relate at a level that means we are never challenged to really enter the world of the other person and, as Paul urges, to rejoice when they rejoice and mourn with them in their time of grief (Rom. 12:15).

Isn't it time to obey the radical call to community?

Questions for Community Reflection

1. What can we learn from the early days of the church about what it means to be a community of faith?
2. What might it mean in your community of faith if there was no one whose need was not met?
3. What is your response to all the questions posed in the section 'The Radical Call to Community' at the end of this chapter?

13

No Barriers at All

*'If reconciliation between peoples and cultures is not happening,
the Gospel's truth is not being confirmed in that place'*
– John Howard Yoder[85]

Gabriel Snyman is a minister in a white-only Dutch Reformed
church in a small town called Delmas in South Africa. One
day he met Toko and Anathi, two Oasis staff, and over a meal
listened to their explanation of a tool Oasis uses to express
the inclusive love of God. Gabriel left that meal with notes
he had made on a paper napkin and from there began a
year-long journey with Oasis to discover more. It wasn't long
before this new understanding he was gaining was tested in
the reality of daily life.

One day he received a phone call requesting his immediate
presence at a house belonging to a member of his congregation.
When he arrived and saw police vehicles outside the house,
he realized that something serious had happened. The house
belonged to a 67-year-old lady who ran a baby day-care centre
there. She, as well as a 5-month-old baby, had been brutally
murdered. Gabriel was able to comfort family members,
especially the baby's parents, and attend to the media.

The murder suspect turned out to be the garden worker, who was a black man, and racism flared up as a result. Gabriel and some companions organized a night vigil at the scene later that week. Community members were given a chance to mourn. This eased the tension temporarily, but the next week this progress was undone by a group of far-right-wing protestors from outside the community who organized a march with racist rhetoric. In front of the municipal buildings they burnt the new South African flag, a symbol of reconciliation in South Africa. Even though only two local community members participated in this march, black people saw it as something conveying how the white people in Delmas felt about them and that, in turn, made the white people even angrier.

In Delmas there were good relationships between black and white pastors. A meeting was called together with the mayor and they wrote and agreed on a statement that declared that both white and black condemned the violence against these unfortunate victims and other victims of crime in their community. As a counteraction to the right-wing march a peaceful march was organized and the new South African flag was raised as a sign of commitment to reconciliation and peace. The mayor read the agreed statement with black and white church leaders by her side. Afterwards a black–white chain of prayer was formed with over three hundred community members from all races, socio-economic classes and backgrounds.

Following this, Gabriel received hate mail and death threats from right-wing extremists. One Sunday he preached a message on reconciliation, during which a notorious right-wing leader, with others, entered his church. Gabriel feared that this leader was armed but politely requested him to take a seat and assured him that he would talk with him and his group afterwards. Fortunately, after they had shared their grievances the group left peacefully.

Since the double murder, nerves have been calmed and various other peace and reconciliation initiatives have taken place. The mother of the murdered baby recently found out that she was pregnant with twins. Gabriel now says that, without a new understanding of how passionate God is about inclusion, his response in these circumstances would have been entirely different.

The central characters in the unfolding drama of the book of Acts were Paul and Peter. In fact, it was an experience that Peter had, recorded in Acts 10, which formed a turning point in the mission of the early church. Up until that point the disciples had not really grasped that the good news was for all people, not just the Jews. However, God gave Peter a vision which coincided with the arrival of non-Jewish visitors at the home where he was staying, and all that changed. Peter went with the visitors to Cornelius, who himself had had a vision in which he had been told by an angel to send for Peter and whose servants it was who had been at Peter's door. The supernatural circumstances around this appointment were undeniable evidence of God at work, so Peter responded, 'I now realise how true it is that God does not show favouritism but accepts from every nation the one who fears him and does what is right' (Acts 10:34, 35).

This was a turning point of seismic proportions. In fact, when the rest of the disciples heard that Peter had been in the home of a non-Jew and had eaten with those present, they were upset. As we have already seen, whom you eat with is very important. Peter had a chance to defend himself and when he explained the circumstances of how it all came about, they all realized that God's purposes were all-inclusive and that non-Jews were to be a part of God's new era of shalom. Shalom was, in fact, what Peter communicated to Cornelius and all of the non-Jews in his home as he shared the gospel with them.

As we read much of what Paul wrote to the churches scattered throughout Asia Minor, it only really makes sense when we understand that the inclusion of non-Jews within the church as equal members precipitated a number of questions. The most significant of these was whether a Gentile had to first become a Jew in order to be a Christian.

Uniting Jews and Non-Jews – At Last!

As Gentiles were added to the church community huge challenges abounded, not least because of the long and ancient history of political enmity between Jews and Gentiles. Many of the internal difficulties within these small communities were caused by this revolutionary change that brought Jews and non-Jews together. All of a sudden, Jewish and Gentile followers of Jesus were crossing the thresholds of each other's homes and eating meals together. They were becoming one as the body of Christ. This was not only a challenge to believers, it was also a witness to the world. It demonstrated God's power to break down the walls of prejudice that divide people. Indeed, it remains core to our witness in the world today.

In one of his letters Paul mentions a 'dividing wall of hostility' (Eph. 2:14). He was very likely alluding to an actual wall or balustrade that prevented Gentiles from entering the main section of the temple in Jerusalem. That wall still existed when Paul wrote his letter and was only physically destroyed in AD 70 when Jerusalem was besieged and the entire temple destroyed by the Romans.

For Paul, the church represented a new social reality in which hate, revenge, oppression, violence and discrimination were replaced by shalom between Jews and Gentiles. For 'two peoples, two cultures, two histories have come to flow into one new humanity, a new creation'.[86] As people and households then joined the church they were not simply giving assent to intellectual beliefs, they were choosing a radical new lifestyle which reflected Jesus' emphasis on inclusion and the indiscriminate nature of true love.

The church became the community where the biggest barriers in the world were broken down. It was the environment of healing and forgiveness. It was the place where love was all-inclusive. Practising the way of Jesus has therefore always involved breaking down barriers with those who are different from us and entering their world, while welcoming them into our own.

This was so important to Paul that he spoke in the most uncompromising terms about some Jewish Christians, including Barnabas, who had stopped sharing meals with uncircumcised Gentile Christians at Antioch (Gal. 2:11, 13). For Paul, it was not an act of shared meal tables that was at stake here. For him, what mattered was the damage this act was doing to a new society that in turn demonstrated

God's purposes of reconciliation for the church and the whole world.[87]

Indiscriminate Relationships

There are a lot of references in Paul's letters to the importance of loving relationships. This love was expressed through the breaking down of dividing walls between ethnic groups, as we have just seen. Other communities in the ancient world were characterized by loving relationships, to be sure. In some cases, as with the Essenes, people even held property in common. The difference in the church was the *indiscriminate* nature of the love among people. As John Zizioulas says, 'Whereas the Jew based the unity of their gatherings on race (or, in the later years, on a broader religious community based on this race) and the pagans with their *collegia* on profession, the Christians declared that in Christ "there is neither Jew nor Greek", "male or female", adult or child, rich or poor, master or slave, etc.'[88]

There is something deeply compelling about the coming together of people who are different from each other. Anyone who watched the 2012 London Olympics could not fail to be moved when competitors of different colour and language embraced each other in the midst of intense competition. The closing ceremony, during which athletes from all countries mingled in joyful celebration, was an enduring sign of what the church should be like. It was hard not to be inspired by this spectacle of community, knowing that even those representing countries that were at war were able to join hands with each other for this brief period.

Wider Inclusion and Reconciliation

It was obstacles not only between Jews and Gentiles but between all groups that needed to be broken down if the new community of the church was to demonstrate to the world that a new era had dawned. This is why Paul passed effortlessly between theological discourse and the practical everyday relationships that people's lives were built around. These were relationships between slaves and masters, parents and children, and husbands and wives.

For the church to be the church these relationships had to be reordered around the inclusive love for all that Jesus had shown to the world and which was now to be the sign among his followers that a new era in history had begun. For it was in the relational life of the community of faith that a clear distinction was to be made between the way the church ordered its relationships and the way the wider culture did. That wider cultural context taught that men were in control; that women and children were second-class citizens; and that those with wealth and power had the right, simply because of their position, to expect loyalty and submission from those not so privileged. The church was called to be different. It was called to be a counter-cultural, alternative community.

Jesus had challenged the assumptions of the world by giving honour to women, welcoming children in a way that profoundly went against societal norms, and by announcing good news for the poor. Yet his approach to the issues of status and place within society was not one of revolution but rather of quiet subversion. Perhaps it was because of this precedent that Paul did not seek a revolutionary reordering of relationships either, but instead encouraged a path that would allow people to relate differently to each other within the church community, while not alienating those outside.

This is an area of struggle today for many of us. Why did Paul not forthrightly denounce slavery when it is clear from the overall themes of Scripture that the subjugation of any human being is not what God intends? I think John Howard Yoder's explanation sheds real light on this. He argues that for Paul to suggest that children, wives and slaves should subordinate themselves, there must have been an alternative thought in their mind. After all, subordination was what was expected within society so there would have been no reason for Paul to address this topic unless an alternative idea was brewing within their consciences. As he says:

> There must have been something in their experience of their becoming Christians, or in their education as new members of the Christian community, or in their experience in the life of that group, which had given to these subjects a vision or a breath of a new kind of dignity and responsibility. This must have already occurred if they were tempted to rise above their station. Only if something in the life or preaching of the church had given them the idea that their subordinate status had been challenged or changed would there be any temptation to the kind of unruliness to which these texts are addressed.[89]

A Subversive Approach

There are real differences between Paul's teaching on subordination and what was normative in the wider cultural context. In that wider context, people unwillingly submitted to their husbands, masters and parents. Paul's instruction was that women, slaves and children should *willingly* subordinate themselves (Eph. 5:21 – 6:9). This indicates that they felt they now had a choice because of the freedom, grace and human dignity offered in the gospel. When Paul advocated 'willing submission', this was not a call to compromise but to subversion.

This is not all, for there were two additional things that made what Paul was saying a challenge to the norms of the wider society. The first was that the motivation for such subordination was not at all related to status or place in society. Rather, it was related to the person's allegiance to their Master Jesus Christ and to their allegiance to their new community – a community in which the ethics of the kingdom of heaven required an alternative imagination.

The second was that alongside the encouragement for 'willing subordination' was the radical mandate to men, parents and masters to embrace the kind of mutuality that could only come from a church culture of equity, freedom and dignity of all. Mutual submission was in fact as revolutionary as you could get. In spite of that, however, Paul was not inciting a fast-burn revolution. He was actually inspiring a slow-burn subversion of the world's systems of relationships. Many of the relationships Paul was addressing were those that existed with people outside the church community. As Christians began to apply the ethic of 'willing submission' in their relationships with non-Christian slave masters, husbands and parents, this would lead to a subversive rather than a revolutionary approach that in the long run would be far more effective in its witness in the world.

Paul certainly did not shy away from letting Christian slave masters know that they needed to reorder their own relationships with their slaves, however badly their slaves behaved. Their submission to Christ meant that they were called to create a totally new dynamic that stood in contrast to cultural expectations. This is one reason why Paul's letter to Philemon was included in the canon of Scripture. In it Paul is at his most persuasive as he urges Philemon to treat his runaway slave Onesimus as a brother and welcome him as if he were welcoming Paul himself.

Communities of Shalom

As Paul wrote to the communities of faith spread around Asia, many of which he had had a hand in starting, his language reflected an understanding of God's purpose for people to experience life in community in all its fullness. He wanted these communities to receive what Israel was meant to receive – shalom. The church was now the community in which God's promises to Israel – including the promise of peace – could be actualized. It was this overriding sense of God's purposes for Christian community that caused Paul to use such passionate rhetoric at times in his letters.

When Paul wrote to the church in Corinth to challenge them about some of their communal practices he seemed really upset. To understand what Paul says in 1 Corinthians 11 we have to realize that worship meetings occurred in people's homes and frequently involved eating meals together.[90] That is why one of the gifts required by those in leadership is that of hospitality. You can't be a leader in God's community without being a person of welcome. It is also why Jesus ministered so often at meal tables. In many ways, as we have already seen, these meals were the message. By eating with outcasts Jesus showed that God's purposes of life were available for all. His open meal tables were signs that the kingdom of God is a kingdom of embrace not exclusion.

No wonder that Paul was upset when the church in Corinth lost sight of such inclusivity. Instead of waiting and sharing, those who had didn't share with those who were poorer but instead consumed in excess (11:21). Their eating and drinking in an 'unworthy' manner (v. 27) was not because they hadn't stopped for a time of personal introspection and confession of sin. It was rather because they had excluded others in the context of this new community. As Paul said, they needed to wait for each other and 'all eat together' (11:33), because the communal meal was the experience of newly defined relationships in a loving, supportive community. If that was not present, the administration of bread and wine would lose its real significance.

The reference to not recognizing the 'body of Christ' in verse 29 is a reference to giving proper honour and respect to the Christ-centred community of faith. As Robert Banks says, 'When these [attitudes to one another] do not reflect the Christ-like pouring out of their lives for each other that lies at the heart of the meal, they are "guilty of drinking the cup and eating the bread in an unworthy manner." '[91]

When the New Testament church remembered Jesus' giving of his body and blood for the salvation of the world as part of their meals together it must have had a profound impact on all present. For in their midst were people who formerly had been enemies – Jews and Gentiles; slaves and those who owned them. As the bread and wine were taken, no one could have missed their significance in relation to how they needed to give their lives in sacrificial love for each other. Reflecting on life in the church in the second century, John Zizioulas makes the point that their Communion services were far more about a demonstration of the reality of God's new community both in the present and in the future than they were about remembering the past.[92]

In our churches today we need to rediscover the sacrament of Holy Communion as a communal act declaring that every wall has been broken down and all hostility is gone. In its place the inclusive, redemptive and life-giving love of Jesus is poured into our hearts. As such, Holy Communion becomes a sign of our holy community.

So, for Paul, radical community was the central characteristic of the church and 'the communities of the Spirit that Paul nurtured turned society upside-down and inside-out – they brought diverse groups together in unity, gave greater honour to those who usually got less and practised equality with one another'.[93]

Breaking Down Barriers Today

Trevor Hudson has spent much of his time trying to help the rich and privileged of South Africa enter into the world of the oppressed and be people who become givers and receivers of forgiveness. In this divided and apartheid-ridden society he realized that reconciliation and forgiveness would only really occur if people were exposed to the world of the other side. So he began to take groups into the communities of the oppressed and create opportunities for friendships to flourish as dividing walls were broken down.

Such experiences have been transformative for many people. He says, 'We would come as pilgrims, not as tourists; as learners, not as teachers; as receivers, not as givers; as listeners, not as talkers.'[94] The result of such encounters is transformative for those engaged in them as they see the strongholds of discrimination replaced by a mindset of empathy and a lifestyle of solidarity. As Trevor says, 'If our communion with God isolates us from the painful realities of our world, inoculates us against feeling the pain of our neighbors, and leads us into excessive preoccupation with our own well-being, it must be considered suspect.'[95]

The Challenge before Us

By definition, the church is the place where all the barriers that exist between people in the world are broken down. It is the place of inclusion and love. The idea of building homogenous congregations that focus only on one race, age group or class is not a biblical one. The idea of the church modelling how rich and poor, old and young, and black and white embrace each other in their differences most definitely is.

The idea of individualized and personalized faith that is reflected in the worship, teaching and life of many local congregations today would have been anathema to Paul. For him, the church was called to be an inclusive community where all the barriers that remained intact in the world were broken down and where justice and equity were practised.

For Paul, Christianity was much more 'we'-centred than 'me'-centred.

This is one of our biggest challenges today. How can we become known for reaching the outsider and those who are different from us? How do we become truly inclusive? How do our liturgy and worship reflect community rather than individualized spirituality? How does loving support of others reflect our very nature rather than being an occasional activity?

Questions for Community Reflection

1. How might the above understanding of 1 Corinthians 11 make our Communion and Eucharist services more meaningful?

2. Do you agree that Paul is encouraging a subversive strategy for changing society – one of evolution rather than revolution? What application might this have for us today?

3. Can you see the theme of community more clearly in Paul's writings in the light of this chapter? What difference might that make?

14

Extending the Circle

'Hostility destroys community. Hospitality restores community.
A divine society, incarnating the trinity in community, is the
creation of a free, friendly, safe space' – Dave Andrews[96]

Seven years ago Arnie and Chantel Swiegers moved into
Cosmo City on the outskirts of Johannesburg. Cosmo City
was a new community that was part of a government initiative to mix those who were being rehoused from the informal
settlements with others from a more middle-class background.
Arnie and Chantel began their time there building relationships and getting to know the dynamics and opportunities of
this location.

Some years previously Arnie had initiated a programme to
assist disadvantaged school leavers in continuing their education
at university level. It had been a huge success, so Arnie began to
research people's appetite for something similar in Cosmo City.
There was a desire for it, so 'Bridge the Gap' started. At the
same time, Chantel, with a background in health, recognized
some of the health needs within the community and began a
programme to train local-community health workers in taking
responsibility for specific parts of the community.

Both of these initiatives and others that were started revolved around the core values of inclusion, empowerment, relationship and equality of all people, values that we espouse in Oasis. Their desire was not to run programmes but to play their part in the establishment of a community that reflected a holistic and biblical understanding of the gospel.

The geographic community existed, but strengthening bonds between black and white, rich and poor, meant addressing issues of trust, justice and opportunity. Only that would ensure that the geographic community became a true community.

If you talk to Arnie and Chantel about their strategy they will mention two things. The first is an approach which encompasses all the programmes: the 'change agent approach'. It is a strategy to empower people within the community to bring change through their own areas of passion and concern. The second is called 'rhythm of life', which articulates a holistic spirituality and which is the foundational reflective process that enables people to remain rooted in their relationships with each other, God, their environment and the wider community.

The result of developing the 'change agent' and 'rhythm of life' approaches has been amazing. There is now a core community of close to a hundred people who meet regularly to embody what it means to follow the path of Jesus, modelling inclusivity, justice and equity. There are Adri-Marie, Scotch, Anathi, Loveness and so many others. The community includes black and white, rich and poor.

The bonds between those who have chosen to walk this path in relationship together are very strong. At the same time the boundaries are very weak between the core group and others who are on the fringes and who, all the time, are being drawn in. Everyone is welcome.

This is not a service-centred church where people come to get fed and watered. It's not an outreach or missional church where people do things for others to win them over. It's not even an attractional church where people come because they like what is going on. Rather, it is a loving, supportive community made up of black and white, rich and poor, those who have come out of the red-light area and those who still work there. It's a community of the broken finding life together. It's a community where God is present among them.

When we grasp the revolutionary nature of the church as a community in which barriers are broken down, possessions are shared, justice is practised and love is the key characteristic of relationships, we begin to ask how the circle can be extended to all people.

When we grasp that the gospel embraces the full-orbed and multi-dimensional purposes of God and is about welcoming people into this new community, we begin to ask questions about the nature and role of evangelism as practised by the church in much of the world today.

Understanding the Term 'Church'

One of the biggest factors shaping our understanding of church is what has become the most common interpretation of the Greek word *ekklesia*. This is the term used by Jesus in Matthew 16:18 as well as on occasions by Paul. Most commentators argue that this means 'called out' – a translation which has led local congregations to build their self-understanding on becoming separate from the community in which they are located. Dave Andrews, in his book *Divine Society*, suggests that this is a misunderstanding. He explains that the original term was used for a local community council that would take time out from their community. The reason they would take this time aside was not to be separate but to think and plan for how they could 'promote the welfare of their locality'.[97]

Holding a 'called-out' theology, the church in many parts of the world has become more like a retreat centre than a community council. This has been derived from a perceived mandate to disengage from its responsibility for those who are part of the local community in which it is situated. The focus has been on preserving the differences between those in the church and those who are not on the same pilgrimage. Yet this ethic of separation stands in complete contrast to so much of the rest of Scripture where we are encouraged as God's children to stand up for justice and peace for all people, not just Christians. In that regard the understanding of *ekklesia* that Dave Andrews states makes so much more sense.[98] The church is a community of people who are tasked to seek the welfare of their community.

When John writes in his first letter to encourage the community of Christ-followers not to love the world (1 John 2:15), he is not urging a separation from people who might contaminate them. Rather, he is urging them not to be sucked into the self-seeking consumerism reflected in continual craving and the boasting which results when people get what they desire.

These are deceptions that entrap people; they do not bring about God's purpose of fullness of life. John is therefore not encouraging a separation from people or from community; he is suggesting a separation from patterns of thought and behaviour that will lead people away from life as God intends.

The Nature of Evangelism

An 'evangel' in the context of New Testament times was a herald – someone who announced good news. This word was not a new Christian term. In the Roman world the evangel would announce the good news of battles won and victories secured. This 'good news' would be announced with a lot of pomp and splendour and the herald would be rather like our modern-day PR director, ensuring that the message was known throughout the empire.

As Christian preachers of the good news spoke to the Jewish community, their message was about how Israel's hopes had been fulfilled in Jesus. As the message was declared to the Greek community it was often framed in the context of how the walls of hostility between Jew and Gentile had been broken down and how the Jewish Messiah was the Saviour of the whole world.

How does our understanding of *ekklesia* help us to understand the evangelistic task of the church? If *ekklesia* in the Christian sense means a community dedicated to the welfare of their locality, it affects everything. Instead of asking how we get people to join us, the key question is how we can be a blessing to those who live in our local community. If we continue to focus on attendance at services and on trying to increase the numbers of people who come to them, we will fail in declaring the multi-dimensional good news of Christ. Sadly, we seem to find it almost impossible to shake off this old paradigm of evangelism. While there are some really wonderful new shoots of encouragement happening in terms of community engagement, there is still a far greater amount of activity designed to elicit an individual response to a spiritual message. This is true of the seeker-sensitive movement and others like it. Local congregations try to become attractive to outsiders by changing the packaging and ensuring that people feel comfortable enough to enter the church building while the central message remains the same.

Although a lot of books are written on the church, most of them are all pointed towards the same end: how do we get more individuals to commit their lives to Christ so that the church will grow numerically? We have all kinds of courses now that lead people to the point where they have enough understanding of the Christian faith to make an informed decision. It's all geared to the individual. Now, for an individual to make a decision to follow Jesus is a good thing. However, if the way faith is portrayed to people is itself individualistic, and I am placed at the centre, this will inevitably produce individualistic disciples.

I believe that when Jesus' life, death and resurrection are communicated in the context of God's purposes for bringing justice, peace and reconciliation to our world, people's perception of the good news will change. Decisions to follow Christ and his way will not be shaped so much on an acceptance of propositional truth, but on the understanding that

God's purposes for all people are good and that his way of bringing these purposes to pass is our only real option.

God Is For Us

One of the biggest obstacles in communicating this multi-dimensional gospel is the fact that many people think God is against them because they are sinners. Somehow we have to help others realize that God's purpose is that we enjoy fullness of life, and that this comes as we rediscover that we were made for the joy of living in a community of people who practise love, justice and peace and who know God as present among them.

In this context, instead of understanding sin in terms of wrong choices made in isolation, we begin to view it as everything that keeps people from wholesome relationships with each other and with God. Sin has to do with those injustices which keep us apart more than personal moral lapses.[99]

In our work among those who are poor and excluded our message is that God is on their side. It stems from an understanding that they need to grasp how God's good purposes mean justice for the oppressed, rather than thinking the oppressed person's first response to the gospel is to confess their personal sin. This is because God is most definitely for them and that is based on the fact that the most profound thing about being human is that we are made in God's image, a truth that is found on the very first page of the Bible before the entry of sin into the world. That paradigm, I believe, is the lens through which we should view all people, for how we view people will determine how we engage with them, which in turn will determine what the outcome will be.[100]

A Community of Difference

In my studies a number of years ago I was introduced to a missional concept called 'the homogenous unit principle'. This was originally proposed by Donald McGavran but was taken up by many other proponents of church growth. The principle said that people are most likely to become Christians among people who are similar to themselves. Now that may be true, but I do not believe that our strategy for growing the church should be built around it. My personal belief is that without the church modelling inclusivity in the face of divisions in the wider community, we cannot be what we are called to be. Growing churches of like-minded people who commit themselves in response to an individualized gospel is not going to usher in God's kingdom built on inclusive love. It's going to take a different kind of church to do that, and that church will be a community of difference, where black and white, rich and poor, literate and those less so, will overcome their differences and prejudices as they create an environment of loving, supportive relationships. Indeed, such communities of difference, where all types of discrimination and cultural bias are broken down, become beacons of light in our increasingly fragmented world.

Our Mission to Make Disciples

This leads us on to another core area that is impacted when we understand community to be central to God's purposes – our mission of making disciples.

When I was growing up, discipleship was purely an individual matter characterized by a number of disciplines such as prayer and Bible study. The teaching I received was centred around achieving holiness through personal confession and forgiveness. It wasn't that this was wrong; it was just that there were some gaps. Never was anything mentioned about the poor or issues of justice. Neither did I hear about the nature of the church as the community where walls of division were broken down.

However, with a new understanding of the multi-dimensional gospel we can now make multi-dimensional disciples who embrace the whole of life as God's domain. That includes the central areas of justice, freedom and release for the oppressed in our world, as well as engagement in caring for the whole of God's creation.

Does this mean that the pursuit of holiness is now no longer relevant in our lives? Not at all. It just means that we understand sin in a far wider sense and we deal with it in community rather than on our own. Instead of me trying to fight my self-rule in isolation, it means fighting it in a community where broken and flawed people are loved and accepted.

One of the words that would be on the lips of someone in the church every week when I was a child was 'sanctification'. It was the word used to describe how I might become more like Jesus. But, as Gilbert Bilezikian says, 'Sanctification cannot be achieved in isolation. It is a community-sustained and directed endeavor . . . A faulty understanding of sanctification as a self-absorbed, private exercise of personal improvement has a fragmenting effect on the church. It must be replaced with a vigorous, holistic doctrine of sanctification that defines it also as the God-given spiritual cement that makes oneness possible.'[101]

An Invitational Community

Key to being effective in mission today is the ability to listen. We need to listen to our neighbours, colleagues and those who live in our communities. We need to be able to discern the deepest cry of their hearts. We need to be able to hear without responding with quick fixes or by pretending that everything becomes rosy when you start to follow Jesus.

When it is time to make an invitation, this does not mean ticking a number of theological boxes. Rather, it means welcoming people into a community of loving, supportive and just relationships. We will invite them to taste and see. Belief may come – indeed it will – but only after belonging. How we act out our beliefs as a community of inclusion will be far more important than any doctrine we declare. For it is through our actions that we will demonstrate the multi-dimensional gospel and the breaking down of barriers that is possible when a community lives 'in Christ'.

Around the world, the walls that divide are still enormously high. People are divided and hostility is expressed around issues of language, culture, race, colour, gender and in a host of other areas besides. How we model equality and inclusivity is fundamental to being the church – it is part of our renewed nature. People from all walks of life, all socio-economic groups and all sexual orientations should find a home in the community of the church. That is our task: to be an invitational community.

A Holistic Approach

For the past thirty or more years there has been an increasing move to what is termed 'holistic ministry' or 'holistic mission'. That in the main has been because the evangelical church, having focused exclusively on evangelism, woke up to the fact that there are many parts of the Bible that encourage the church to engagement among the poor. One such passage is in the book of James that speaks of looking after 'orphans and widows in their distress' (1:27). Those who took the Bible seriously began to realize that evangelism is far more than getting people to repent of sin and believe in Christ. It is also about showing the Father's love for the fatherless and his compassion for the widow.

The trouble with this heralding of a holistic approach is that by its very nature it is seeking to join two areas that should never have been separated in the first place.[102] Evangelism and social action are seen as separate because evangelism is seen as a message of sin and forgiveness that individuals are invited to respond to, while social action is seen as helping those in need. But these two endeavours were never supposed to be prised apart. In Jesus' life and ministry the two were integrated. In the mission of the earliest churches they were integrated too.

By embracing the multi-dimensional view of the gospel I have suggested, when we speak about the good news we tell others about God's purpose for justice, inclusion, community, and liberation for the oppressed as well as about repentance and forgiveness. All of these things are a part of God's good purpose. In addition, we also model and demonstrate what repentance and forgiveness look like, what justice and inclusion look like, and we do that through God's new community, the church.

This is the good news of the kingdom where everyone can come into the centre and find their place, everyone can be forgiven and worship, everyone can play their part as a contributor to God's world, everyone can discover fullness of life, because God's original purpose of right relationship with him and others can come into being.

So we don't need to develop a new idea called 'holistic ministry'. We need to rediscover God's integrated vision articulated throughout the Bible.

The Good News of the Kingdom

All this also means that we need to shift our emphasis from a gospel of salvation to the good news about the kingdom of heaven. The good news of the kingdom is that those who were previously excluded – the poor, crippled, lame and blind – are now welcomed into God's eternal family. It is good news for the poor.

Once evangelism is separated from being 'good news for the poor' it can end up being mono-dimensional, a message for middle-class people to ensure they can have the best of both worlds – a comfortable life now *and* the security of an eternal destiny in heaven. But that is not what God wants.

God does not want us to preach a one-dimensional gospel of personal salvation because that is primarily a message that is limited to the spiritual and concerned mostly with the future. The good news of the kingdom, however, is mostly about God acting right now and covers the whole of our lives because it embraces us in our humanity and our need of relationship with others.

Furthermore, this is really good news for those who are excluded, ostracized and pushed to the edges of our society. In fact, one of the reasons I believe the gospel is about justice and inclusion is that, if it were simply about the spiritual and about the future, it could never have been proclaimed as 'good news' to the poor nor understood as such by them. In order for it to be good news there must have been something in Jesus' proclamation that was attractive to their situation then. The idea that if they believed and trusted in Jesus they would go to heaven would hardly have seemed a message to shout from the rooftops. A message that proclaimed the beginnings of a new community where they would be treated as equals, supported, loved and included would certainly have motivated the crowds of ordinary folk to come out and hear what Jesus had to say.

To come at this from another angle, the importance of justice in the Bible is not an add-on to the gospel; it is a foundational truth within it. The reason that God wants us to act justly, love mercy and walk humbly is because this, by definition, is how his new community operates, and the good news is that those who have suffered oppression or been marginalized or rejected can find their home and their place within it.

Our heralding to those outside the church community is first and foremost the good news of the kingdom which is that, through Christ, all are now welcome to join in and be a part of this new community that is to be a sign to everyone that God's new era has indeed arrived.

The gospel is the gospel of shalom; it is justice; it is forgiveness, reconciliation, bread, water and life. It is God's desire for wholeness, fullness and completeness in all areas as we live with others in community while God dwells among us.

Questions for Community Reflection

1. How would you explain the gospel to someone you were talking with in the light of this book?
2. How can we reorientate ourselves to a new understanding of evangelism, mission and the prophetic, in the light of the Bible's central theme of community?

15

Let Us Be

'Without community, there is no Christianity'
– Gilbert Bilezikian[103]

We began with the beautiful picture of the future that is described in John's vision on the island of Patmos in the last book of the Bible, Revelation. It's a picture of vibrancy, health, hope and joy as God dwells among his people. The last two chapters of the Bible paint this picture not only through the image of God wiping away all tears but also by means of references to so many other aspects of life in the 'New Jerusalem'.

It's a city where those who are thirsty can find that thirst quenched through the spring of the water of life without cost; a city where its brilliance shines like a very precious jewel; a city where the gates are always open and where there is no night because God's continual glory gives it light. It's a city where people are not divided but where relationships are healed and fruit is found in abundance.

Such a vision for John and the churches he was connected to would have been a huge encouragement at a time when persecution was rife. It's also an encouragement to us today that God is not planning to abandon his world and jet his followers off to a new location. In fact, God says 'I am making everything new!' (Rev. 21:5); rather than abandoning the old, God wants to make the old new. God's purposes are accordingly about renewal, restoration and recreation.

God Is Community

In the second chapter we went back to the very beginning and saw that fundamental to being human is the fact that we have been created for relationship with others. Being made in the image of the triune God means that, within the deepest places of our hearts, there is a longing to know and be known.

God is community and, as his image bearers, we find that place of rest only as we live in the midst of loving, supportive relationships that provide the mutuality we need in times of sorrow and of joy.

Indeed, as image bearers of God the need for community is built into our DNA. At the same time, image bearing has placed a responsibility on us within God's creation: to image him in his world. This we do through our stewardship of all God's good gifts and through our loving, supportive relationships that establish communities of shalom.

Having seen that community is crucial to God's purposes at the bookends of the Bible, we then explored this theme within the rest of Scripture.

The Old Testament and Community

In the Old Testament we saw that God chose and sought to form the Israelites into a loving, supportive community that would bless the nations of the world. God gave them the Ten Commandments and other instructions for life that were fundamentally relational; then, through the tabernacle and the temple he made it very clear that he didn't want to be a distant God, but wanted to share their lives and live among them.

The community of Israel was to be a place of goodness, wholeness, completeness and fullness of life for all, summed up in the Hebrew concept of shalom. There were times when Israel seemed to grasp this, but more often than not people on the edges of society were left out and, worse still, were exploited and oppressed by those with power. Unfortunately, the descendants of those who had been oppressed in Egypt and had been rescued from their slavery now became the oppressors of their own people. They continued with their religious rituals but ignored the plight of the poor.

The Community around Jesus

In fact, their failure as a community to be loving, just, inclusive and supportive of all led to a new plan and a new covenant. God decided to send his Son, who would be the 'Prince of shalom' and would gather around him a community of the excluded and broken. That community would seek to live as God had always intended, modelling shalom to the world, with his presence clearly among them. Then the world would see and be drawn in.

As God became flesh at Bethlehem, the first to know this were the shepherds on the hillside. This clearly demonstrated that God's purposes were for all people and particularly those on the edge of society.

When the time was right Jesus went public and modelled and taught what God had always wanted and what a community of shalom really looked like.

There were setbacks, and things didn't always work out the way they might have done, but by the time Jesus was crucified and resurrected his disciples had enough of an idea that they were able to embrace the process of becoming a vibrant, loving, supportive community where there were no people in need. Crucial, of course, was the fact that the power of the resurrection was now available to this new community through God's Spirit that dwelt in and among them.

Paul's Role in the Community of the Church

Essential to the formation and development of the early church was the ministry of the apostle Paul, who had a dramatic conversion and then spent his life establishing small communities of Jesus followers all over Asia Minor. Fundamental to the nature of these communities was the fact that they crossed all the boundaries that divided people within the culture of the time. Most significant was the uniting of Jews and Gentiles, but in addition there were slaves and masters, rich and poor, men and women, parents and children. These were all encouraged to view each other through the new lens of God's inclusive love.

These communities all had their problems but, through his visits and letters, Paul urged them to continue to model to the world God's purpose that all people find fullness and wholeness of life within loving, supportive relationships that were centred around Christ.

The central message of the Bible truly is about community. It's a message that God wants to dwell among us as we nurture relationships which are supportive and just. It's a message that everyone is invited and nobody excluded.

This Framework Brings Freedom

As this framework shapes our understanding of life and faith we become freer as people, as many of the old dichotomies disappear. We no longer need to drive a wedge between evangelism and social action, between the sacred and the secular or between an emphasis on the future rather than the present. This is liberating. We become freed from narrow one-dimensional agendas and can now embrace the multi- dimensional nature of the good news in Christ that is for all people and for the whole of life.

There are an increasing number of theologians as well as community practitioners who are writing about this today and indeed there are some voices that have been expressing this for some time. Francis Schaeffer, one of the greatest thinkers of the twentieth century within the evangelical church, said, 'The Lordship of Christ covers all of life and all of life equally. It is not that true spirituality covers all of life, but it covers all parts of the spectrum of life equally. In this sense there is nothing concerning reality that is not spiritual.'[104]

Yes, our individual response to the claims of Christ is important, but without an understanding of its place within the bigger picture of God's cosmic purposes it has the potential to become so individualistic that it is a pale reflection of the multi-dimensional and all-embracing gospel that Jesus proclaimed.

Living This Out in Our Communities

This paradigm shift is already beginning to occur in a small way within the church in the West. However, we should not think that it will become the norm without some significant battles being won. Some of our existing thinking and practices are rooted so deeply in our imaginations that it will take a lot of persuading to change. That is a theological task, for our imaginations need to be captured by God's all-embracing cosmic redemptive agenda that is rooted in loving community today. At the moment our imaginations are still too often shaped both by an individualized view of faith and a materialist and consumerist agenda that numbs us to the harshness of life for the vast majority of people alive today.

In a sense we have two challenges to face. On the one hand we need to resist the shaping of our lives by a culture that does not reflect the truth that we are all made in God's image. The forces that shape us include individualism, materialism and consumerism. The second challenge we face is to reshape the church around God's multi-dimensional agenda for the renewal of the cosmos rather than around the mono-dimensional agenda of personal salvation.

Although these challenges are big I have a great measure of optimism as we move into the future. That optimism is fuelled by the younger generation who live far more integrated lives than my generation and who have already rejected much of the silo thinking that has wreaked havoc within the Christian community for so long. I believe that this present generation's focus on justice, fairness, equity and care of the earth are all expressions of great hope. Many young people are asking questions of faith that demonstrate an inherent responsibility for others. Some have rejected the church because of its insularity or focus on dogma. None of those that I have met have rejected Jesus. That is why I have hope. If we can grasp that the good news of Jesus is good news for all and is about justice, fairness, equity and peace – the multi-dimensional gospel – then we will see God's kingdom come in places of squalor and despair as well as in locations of economic prosperity. Then those who have given up on church will re-engage too. They will re-engage because we have become a real community, where all boundaries are broken down and where our main task is not simply to sing and listen to preaching but to *be inclusive community together*.

That excites me. I hope it excites you too.

Endnotes

1 Andy Matheson, *In His Image: Understanding and Embracing the Poor* (Milton Keynes: Authentic, 2010).

2 Tom Wright, *Surprised by Hope* (London: SPCK, 2007), p. 117. Used by permission of SPCK.

3 Tim Chester, *A Meal with Jesus: Discovering Grace, Community and Mission around the Table* (Wheaton, IL: Crossway, copyright 2011), p. 71.

4 Perry Yoder, *Shalom: The Bible's Word for Salvation, Justice, and Peace* (Nappanee, IN: Evangel, 1987), p. 49.

5 Steve Chalke and Alan Mann, *Different Eyes: The Art of Living Beautifully* (Grand Rapids, MI: Zondervan, 2010), p. 157. Copyright © 2010 by Steve Chalke. Used by permission of Zondervan. www.zondervan.com

6 Jean Vanier, *Community and Growth* (London: Darton, Longman & Todd, 1979), p. 8.

7 Tim Chester and Steve Timmis. *Total Church: A Radical Reshaping around Gospel and Community.* (Nottingham: IVP, 2007 (pp. 38, 39.

8 Doug P. Baker, *Covenant and Community: Our Role as the Image of God* (Eugene, OR: Wipf & Stock, 2008), p. 72. Used by permission of Wipf and Stock Publishers. www.wipfandstock.com.

9   Kathy Escobar, *Down We Go: Living into the Wild Ways of Jesus* (San Jose, CA: Civitas, 2011), pp. 45, 46.

10 Gregory Boyle, *Tattoos on the Heart: The Power of Boundless Compassion* (New York: Free Press, 2010)

11 Vanier, *Community and Growth*, p. 14.

12 Vanier, *Community and Growth*, p. 59.

13 William P. Young, *The Shack* (London: Hodder & Stoughton, 2008).

14 Jonathan Wilson-Hartgrove, *New Monasticism: What It Has to Say to Today's Church* (Grand Rapids, MI: Brazos Press, 2008), p. 61.

15 Excerpts from Richard Rohr, *Things Hidden: Scripture as Spirituality* (Cincinnati: St. Anthony Messenger Press, 2008), are reprinted by permission of Franciscan Media. All rights reserved. p 113.

16 Scott McKnight, *Embracing Grace: A Gospel for All of Us* (London: SPCK, 2007), p. 90. Used by permission of SPCK.

17 Chris Wright, *Old Testament Ethics for the People of God* (IVP, 2004), p. 363.

18 Scott McKnight, *Embracing Grace: A Gospel for All of Us* (London: SPCK, 2007), p. 66. Used by permission of SPCK.

19 Craig Bartholomew and Michael Goheen, *The Drama of Scripture: Finding our Place in the Biblical Story* (London: SPCK, 2006), p. 153. Used by permission of SPCK.

20 P. Yoder, *Shalom*, p. 52.

21 Mark Greene, *The Best Idea in the World: How Putting Relationships First Transforms Everything* (Grand Rapids, MI: Zondervan, 2009), p. 137. Copyright © 2009 by Mark Greene. Used by permission of Zondervan. www.zondervan.com

22 In his book, *The Church Beyond the Congregation* (Carlisle: Paternoster, 1999), James Thwaites says a lot about how the split-level view was developed through the time of Aquinas and Aristotle and then remained intact through the time of the Reformation.

23 James Torrance, *Worship, Community and the Triune God of Grace* (Downers Grove, IL: IVP, 1996), p. 37.

24 Torrance, *Worship, Community and the Triune God of Grace*, p. 37.

25. Tom Wright, *How God Became King: The Forgotten Story of the Gospels* (London: SPCK, 2012), p. 164. Used by permission of SPCK.

26 Quote from *Living Toward a Vision* by Walter Brueggemann, © 1982 United Church Press. The Pilgrim Press. p. 86. All rights reserved. Used by permission.

27 Thwaites, *The Church Beyond the Congregation*, p. 74.

28 Torrance, *Worship, Community and the Triune God of Grace*, p. 39.

29 Glen Stassen and David Gushee. *Kingdom Ethics: Following Jesus in Contemporary Context* (Downers Grove, IL: IVP Academic, 2003), p. 56.

30 Wilson-Hartgrove *New Monasticism*, p. 64.

31 Excerpts from Richard Rohr, *Things Hidden: Scripture as Spirituality* (Cincinnati: St. Anthony Messenger Press, 2008), are reprinted by permission of Franciscan Media. All rights reserved. p. 58.

32 C. Wright, *Old Testament Ethics for the People of God*, p. 51.

33 Boyle, *Tattoos on the Heart*, p. 31.

34 Tom Wright, *How God Became King: The Forgotten Story of the Gospels* (London: SPCK, 2012), p. 88. Used by permission of SPCK.

35 This is quoted by Jesus in Matthew 12:7 but is originally found in Hosea's prophetic book, chapter 6 verse 6.

36 Wilson-Hartgrove. *New Monasticism*, p. 63.

37 From *Shalom, A Study of the Biblical Concept of Peace*, © 2002 by Donald Gowan. p. 29. Used by permission of The Kerygma Program, All rights reserved.

38 Perry Yoder and Willard Swartley, eds. *The Meaning of Peace* (Louisville: Westminter/John Knox Press, 1992), p. 19.

39 Yoder and Swartley, eds. *The Meaning of Peace*, p. 19.

40 Gowan, *Shalom, A Study of the Biblical Concept of Peace*, pp. 20–22.

41 From *Shalom, A Study of the Biblical Concept of Peace*, © 2002 by Donald Gowan. p 24. Used by permission of The Kerygma Program, All rights reserved.

42 Tim Chester, *A Meal with Jesus: Discovering Grace, Community and Mission around the Table* (Wheaton, IL: Crossway, copyright 2011), p. 121.

43 P. Yoder, *Shalom*, p. 79.

44 Alan Roxburgh, *Missional: Joining God in the Neighborhood* (Grand Rapids, MI: Baker, 2011), p. 135.

45 P. Yoder, and W. Swartley eds. *The Meaning of Peace*, p. 42, 43.

46 John 1:14; Eugene Peterson, *The Message* (Colorado Springs: NavPress, 2004).

47 John Yoder talks about this in *Body Politics* when discussing Jesus' use of Isaiah 61, from which he reads in the synagogue in Nazareth as recorded in Luke 4. (*Body Politics: Five Practices of the Christian Community Before the Watching World* [Scottdale, PA: Herald Press, 2001], p. 24.)

48 Luke 17:21; Peterson, *The Message*.

⁴⁹ Tim Chester, *A Meal with Jesus: Discovering Grace, Community and Mission around the Table* (Wheaton, IL: Crossway, copyright 2011), p. 15.

⁵⁰ Quote from *Living Toward a Vision* by Walter Brueggemann, © 1982 United Church Press. The Pilgrim Press. p. 76. All rights reserved. Used by permission.

⁵¹ See my book *In His Image*, where I give a fuller explanation of this.

⁵² Dave Andrews, *A Divine Society* (Queensland: Frank Communications, 2008), p. 77. Used by permission of Wipf and Stock Publishers. www.wipfandstock.com

⁵³ Roxburgh, *Missional*, p. 97.

⁵⁴ Gilbert Bilezikian, *Community 101: Reclaiming the Local Church as Community of Oneness* (Grand Rapids, MI: Zondervan, 1997), p. 36. Copyright © Gilbert Bilezikian. Used by permission of Zondervan. www.zondervan.com

⁵⁵ Stassen and Gushee, *Kingdom Ethics*, p. 42.

⁵⁶ Tom Wright, *Matthew for Everyone* (London: SPCK, 2004), p. 36. Used by permission of SPCK.

⁵⁷ Stassen and Gushee, *Kingdom Ethics*, p. 42.

⁵⁸ Stassen and Gushee, *Kingdom Ethics*, p. 42.

⁵⁹ See Wilson-Hartgrove. *New Monasticism*, ch. 4.

⁶⁰ Some people have interpreted Jesus' seeming injunctions – such as never getting angry – as impossible to live up to. However, Stassen and Gushee (*Kingdom Ethics*) point out that in the Greek these are participles and that the command follows afterwards. They have a very helpful table that shows in each of the illustrative points how the command can be seen as a transforming initiative rather than a new impossible benchmark to live up to. For example, in response to the command not to kill, the participle links anger to killing but the new command is

then to overcome this cycle of violence through being proactive in seeking reconciliation.

61 John Howard Yoder, *The Politics of Jesus* (Grand Rapids, MI: Eerdmans, 1994), p. 117.

62 Excerpts from Richard Rohr, *Things Hidden: Scripture as Spirituality* (Cincinnati: St. Anthony Messenger Press, 2008), are reprinted by permission of Franciscan Media. All rights reserved. p. 61.

63 Madhukshi's story is captured among many others in Clare Nonhebel's book *Finding Oasis*, in which she records the stories of many of those Oasis has helped in both Mumbai and Bangalore. (*Finding Oasis: Powerful Stories from the Slums of Mumbai* [Milton Keynes: Authentic, 2010], p. 142.)

64 Vanier, *Community and Growth*, p. 132.

65 Vanier, *Community and Growth*, p. 185.

66 Scott McKnight, *Embracing Grace* (London: SPCK, 2007), p. 64. Used by permission of SPCK.

67 P. Yoder, *Shalom*, p. 121.

68 From *The Son of God in the Roman World*, by Michael Peppard (2012). By permission of Oxford University Press. p. 92.

69 Robert Banks, *Paul's Idea of Community: The Early House Churches in Their Cultural Setting* (Peabody, MA: Hendrickson, 1994), p. 190.

70 From *Shalom, A Study of the Biblical Concept of Peace*, © 2002 by Donald Gowan. p. 65. Used by permission of The Kerygma Program, All rights reserved.

71 Brian Walsh and Sylvia Keesmat, *Colossians Remixed: Subverting the Empire* (Downers Grove, IL: IVP, 2004), pp. 83, 84.

72 This is how Walsh and Keesmat (*Colossians Remixed*) express it as part of their reflection on the contrast between Pax Romana and Paul's vision of the kingdom.

73 Scott McKnight, *Embracing Grace: A Gospel for All of Us* (London: SPCK, 2007), p. 90. Used by permission of SPCK.

74 Banks, *Paul's Idea of Community*, p. 59.

75 From *Body Politics* by John Howard Yoder. © 1992, Herald Press: Scottdale, PA 15683. p. 17. Used by permission.

76 I first heard this expression used for the creation of a deacons committee by Joel Edwards at a meeting in London.

77 From *Body Politics* by John Howard Yoder. © 1992, Herald Press: Scottdale, PA 15683. p. 32. Used by permission.

78 Wayne Meeks, *The First Urban Christians: The Social World of the Apostle Paul* (New Haven: Yale University Press, 1983), p. 88.

79 Meeks provides a good overview of how households were organized and how they functioned at the time of the early church in *The First Urban Christians*.

80 Banks. *Paul's Idea of Community*, pp. 26, 27.

81 Banks. *Paul's Idea of Community*, p. 108.

82 This is mentioned by John Howard Yoder in his introduction to *Body Politics*.

83 Peterson, *The Message*.

84 Scott McKnight, *Embracing Grace: A Gospel for All of Us* (London: SPCK, 2007), p. 73. Used by permission of SPCK.

85 From *Body Politics* by John Howard Yoder. © 1992, Herald Press: Scottdale, PA 15683. p. 38. Used by permission.

86 From *Body Politics* by John Howard Yoder. © 1992, Herald Press: Scottdale, PA 15683. p. 30. Used by permission.

87 See Meeks, *The First Urban Christians*, p. 161.

88 John D. Zizioulas, *Being As Communion: Studies in Personhood and the Church* (London: Darton, Longman & Todd, 2004), p. 151.

[89] J.H. Yoder, *The Politics of Jesus*. p. 173.

[90] Tim Chester explains how church meetings were actually meals in *A Meal with Jesus*, p. 54, and how central eating was in the life of the early church.

[91] Banks. *Paul's Idea of Community*, p. 83.

[92] Zizioulas. *Being As Communion*, p. 152.

[93] Andrews, *A Divine Society*, p. 100. Used by permission of Wipf and Stock Publishers. www.wipfandstock.com

[94] From *A Mile in My Shoes: Cultivating Compassion* by Trevor Hudson. © 2005. p. 18. Used by permission of Upper Room Books®. books.upperroom.org.

[95] From *A Mile in My Shoes: Cultivating Compassion* by Trevor Hudson. © 2005. p. 71. Used by permission of Upper Room Books®. books.upperroom.org.

[96] Andrews. *A Divine Society* p. 154. Used by permission of Wipf and Stock Publishers. www.wipfandstock.com

[97] Andrews. *A Divine Society*, p. 105. Used by permission of Wipf and Stock Publishers. www.wipfandstock.com

[98] John Howard Yoder in *Body Politics*, p. 2, makes the same point when he references the business that would have been done in a town meeting on behalf of all of the society around.

[99] Stassen and Gushee, *Kingdom Ethics*, p. 345, explain how the overwhelming emphasis in the Bible is around community-restoring justice when the number of references are compared with references to sexual sin which has often been highlighted within the church.

[100] This is a subject I deal with in some depth in my first book, In His Image.

[101] Gilbert Bilezikian, *Community 101: Reclaiming the Local Church as Community of Oneness* (Grand Rapids, MI: Zondervan,

1997), p. 62. Copyright © Gilbert Bilezikian. Used by permission of Zondervan. www.zondervan.com

[102] Many people have written about this. The work of John Stott was seminal, especially around the time of the Lausanne Conference in 1974. His book *Issues Facing Christians Today* (Grand Rapids, MI: Zondervan, 4th edn., 2006) is worth reading on this. World Vision have a lot of publications on the topic and anything by Bryant Myers is also especially worth reading.

[103] Gilbert Bilezikian, *Community 101: Reclaiming the Local Church as Community of Oneness* (Grand Rapids, MI: Zondervan, 1997), p. 35. Copyright © Gilbert Bilezikian. Used by permission of Zondervan. www.zondervan.com

[104] Francis A. Schaeffer, *A Christian Manifesto* (Wheaton, IL: Crossway, 1981), p. 19.

Réseau Michée
Rede Miquéias
Red Miqueas
Micah Network

Micah Network is a global Christian networking bringing together people who are passionate about Integral Mission. The key attributes that Micah brings are:

- Global: bringing together people from around the world is essential as the various cultures, contexts and perspectives enriches our discussions and helps unpack the issues we face together
- Inclusive: bringing together Christian initiatives such as aid and mission organizations, Bible colleges and seminaries, local church, and business as mission helps to hear one another and work towards an integrated approach to community transformation
- Theology and practice: ensuring that theology and practice are brought together underpins all we share and learn together
- Integral discipleship: learning and growing together to live a missional lifestyle and apply integral mission in and through all we do together
- Justice: recognizing that the very character of God is one of justice means that as we reflect Jesus in our communities we need to reflect his character of justice together.

In all of the above what stands out is the recognition that we are better together, the impact is deeper and fuller.
Andy Matheson's book *We Not Me* captures this truth and we are thrilled to stand with him and the message he shares.

In His Image

Understanding and Embracing the Poor

Andy Matheson

You've heard the overwhelming statistics. You've probably felt compassion, guilt, powerlessness, hopelessness. You might have given money, food, clothes, or even some of your time to help a few of the billions of people living in destitution in our world. But have you actually engaged with someone, another human being created in the image of God, who is dying in the arms of poverty? Andy Matheson argues that we can only begin to understand poverty, its effects, and possible solutions, when we focus on the truth that all people are made in God's image. God calls us to meet with the poor not primarily to offer services or to develop programmes, but to develop relationships and to show God's love.

978-1-85078-870-6

Distinctives

Dare to Be Different

Vaughan Roberts

In a fresh and readable style, the author of *Turning Points*, Vaughan Roberts, issues a challenging call to Christians to live out their faith. We should be different from the world around us – Christian distinctives should set us apart in how we live, think, act and speak.

Targeting difficult but crucial areas such as our attitude to money and possessions, sexuality, contentment, relativism and service, this is holiness in the tradition of J.C. Ryle for the contemporary generation. Roberts helps us to consider how we are to respond biblically to the temptations and pitfalls surrounding us – giving what we cannot keep to gain what we cannot lose.

978-1-85078-331-2

TRUE WORSHIP

What is the Nature of
True Christian Worship?

VAUGHAN ROBERTS

True Worship

*Vaughan
Roberts*

What is the nature of true Christian worship? What are we actually doing when we meet together for 'church' on Sundays? And how does that connect with what we do the rest of the week?

Vaughan Roberts answers these questions and more as he brings readers back to the Bible in order to define what worship is and isn't, what it should and shouldn't be. While we may struggle to define worship by arguing about singing hymns with the organ versus modern songs with guitars and drums, or about the place of certain spiritual gifts, Roberts suggests we are asking the wrong questions. For true worship is more than this – it is to encompass the whole of life. This book challenges us to worship God every day of the week, with all our heart, mind, soul and strength.

978-1-85078-445-6

This World

Playground or Battleground?

A. W. Tozer

There was a time, Tozer writes, when our Christian forebears saw the world as it truly is: a battlefield. They knew that hell is a force pitted against God, heaven and righteousness. Tozer fears that now people think of the world as a playground, not a battleground. He exhorts us to appreciate the seriousness of the spiritual struggle we are all engaged in, but also to see it as a battle in which victory is certain.

978-1-85078-201-8

Authentic

We trust you enjoyed reading this book
from Authentic Media. If you want to be
informed of any new titles from this author
and other exciting releases you can sign up
to the Authentic newsletter online:

authenticmedia.co.uk

Contact us:

by post:
Authentic Media
52 Presley Way
Crownhill
Milton Keynes
MK8 0ES

E-mail:
info@authenticmedia.co.uk

Follow us: